SPEAKING

STUDENT'S BOOK

ENGLISH FOR ACADEMIC STUDY SERIES

SPEAKING

Student's Book

Mark Rignall and Clare Furneaux

PRENTICE HALL
EUROPE

The form in which this material is now being published is the outcome of a cycle of trialling and evaluation at the University of Reading, UK, from 1993 to 1996. We are extremely grateful to the many students and teachers at the Centre for Applied Language Studies who contributed to this process. Amongst the teachers were: Lesley Archer, Jon Blundell, Elaine Brown, Irwin Buchanan, Rosemary Dorey, Irene Guy, Sylvia Haworth, Wendy Mallas, Joan McCormack, Clare McCullagh, Deborah Sayer, Ellen Singleton, John Slaght, Sue Weakley and Rachel Woodward. Simon Hunt, who contributed task 3.5 on pages 26 and 27, Steve Miller, Anne Pallant and Alan Tonkyn were particularly generous with their feedback.

We would like to thank the following students and members of staff from other departments who contributed in various ways: Mike Deadman (Crop Protection Research Unit), Barry Jones (Graduate School of European and International Studies), Jim Murray (Department of Construction Management), David Ansell (Agricultural Economics), Chris Grose, Lee Ying, Yoshiko Nagano and Umit Unal.

The authors and publishers would also like to thank the following for permission to reproduce copyright material in this book:
BBC English for extracts from *Britain Now* © Catherine Addis (1992), published by the British Broadcasting Corporation, in The family in Britain Text B; Channel Four Television for extracts from *Faces of the Family* by Tobe Aleksander (1994) in The Family in Britain Text A; Marion Geddes, Gill Sturtridge and Sheila Been for the adaptation of *Advanced Conversation* (1991), page 11: Your attitudes to speaking English; *New Scientist* for extracts from 'Roll up for the Telepathy Test' by John McCrone (15 May 1993); Northcote House/How to Books for the adaptation of stages in settling into a new environment taken from 'How to study and live in Britain' by Jane Woolfenden (1990).

First published in 1997 by
Prentice Hall Europe
A division of Prentice Hall International (UK) Ltd
Campus 400, Spring Way
Maylands Avenue, Hemel Hempstead
Hertfordshire, HP2 7EZ

Printed and bound in Great Britain by Biddles Limited, Guildford and King's Lynn

Library of Congress Cataloging in Publication Data

British Library Cataloguing in Publication Data

A catalogue record for this book is available from the British Library

ISBN   013-507591-2

CONTENTS

TABLE OF UNITS

UNIT	TOPIC	SKILLS FOCUS	LANGUAGE HELP
Foundation	You and your course	Exchanging information	Repair expressions
1	Countries	Preparing a presentation	Asking questions after a presentation
2	The home	Preparing for your audience	Describing an object
3	Education	Looking for ideas to shape your talk	Signpost expressions
4	The family	Collecting information	Comparison and contrast Describing trends
5	The media	Giving an overview	Asking for clarification
6	Health	Preparing a group presentation	Expressing proportion
7	Population and migration	Responding to questions	Describing trends Cause and effect Responding to questions
8	Defence	Generating ideas	Expressing opinion Agreeing and disagreeing
9	Parapsychology	Rehearsing and evaluating	Referring to a text Expressing opinion
10	Studying in a new environment	Summarising in discussion	Deduction

INTRODUCTION

Aims of the course

This course is designed for students who are planning to study at a college or university where the language of instruction is English. It aims to help you develop the oral communication skills in English that are needed for academic study. In particular, it will improve your ability to:

- give short oral presentations effectively
- contribute to seminar discussions appropriately and fluently
- follow the contributions made to the discussion by others
- assess your performance in discussion and presentation tasks.

The course is suitable for intermediate and upper-intermediate learners of English; we recommend a minimum starting level of IELTS band 5 or TOEFL 490. It can be used successfully both by people who have little experience of study skills, and also by those who have good study skills in their own language and now need to practise using them in English.

Contents

The course consists of a Foundation Unit followed by ten standard units, all of which provide practice in the kinds of oral communication you will have to carry out in your academic studies. The units refer you to the Language Help section on pages 123-141, which presents key language organised according to function (such as **Describing trends** or **Expressing proportion**). Also at the back of the book is the Independent Learner section on pages 106-122, which is designed to support you in your learning both during and after the course.

   Each unit guides you through a sequence of activities: identifying issues related to the unit topic, extracting relevant information from the texts provided or from other sources, then putting your ideas forward in discussion and/or presentation. This sequence reflects the basic study cycle (see Figure 1 page ix), which students on virtually all academic courses have to follow.

The unit thus provides an authentic context in which you practise exactly the speaking skills you will need for academic study at an English-medium college or university.

The topics that have been selected are accessible and stimulating, but suitable at the same time for the relatively formal, academic-type treatment that you need to practise. The tasks do not require any specialist background knowledge. This allows you to concentrate on skill development without the distraction of highly technical subject-matter.

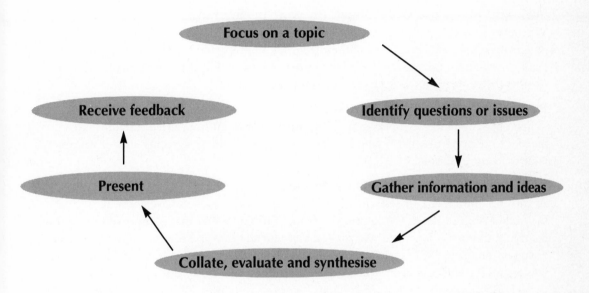

Figure 1: The basic study cycle

How to get the most out of the course

Think about your learning

Take the opportunity in the Foundation Unit and then in the Learner Diary task in each unit (see page 6 for example) to clarify what your needs are in spoken English, how you learn best, how much progress you have made, and what you can do to make further progress.

Think, plan and rehearse for tasks

Prepare for each unit by thinking carefully about the unit topic and identifying questions or issues related to it.

Prepare for listening tasks by asking yourself questions about the topic. Prepare for discussion and presentation tasks by thinking carefully about the task topic, planning what you intend to say, and rehearsing it; this applies to discussions as well as presentations – practise noting down and/or saying, before the discussion starts, the main points you want to make.

Seek and make use of feedback on your performance

Whenever possible, get someone to comment on your performance of discussion and presentation tasks, and make use of their feedback in preparing for your next performance. Both giving and receiving feedback help to develop your skill at self-assessment. You can use the checklists (pages 112,113 and 118) for this purpose.

Be an active listener and speaker

When other students are speaking in a presentation or discussion, listen carefully and prepare to respond to what is said, by questioning, challenging, agreeing and/or making your own contribution.

Keep your language records up to date

At the end of each task or session, ask yourself what language you have come across that you might want to use in the future. Experiment to find a way that is effective (for you) of recording this useful language. We suggest that you add new expressions to the Language Help section (page 123) as you meet them, and keep a separate notebook or file in which you organise your vocabulary according to topic as well as word form.

Make use of language reference books

Make full use of a good English-English dictionary and a reference grammar book. These aids enable you to learn efficiently during the course, and to go on improving independently after the course.

FOUNDATION UNIT: YOU AND YOUR COURSE

SESSION 1

Step 1: Listening

1.1   Listen to your teacher talk about him/herself. Indicate with a tick which of the topic areas below he/she mentions.

TOPIC	MENTIONED?
1. Home town	
2. Family	
3. Education	
4. Leisure interests	
5. Experience of travel overseas	
6. Likes and dislikes (food, music, etc.)	
7. Plans and ambitions	
8. Reasons for becoming a teacher	
9. Professional interests	

Step 2: Introducing yourself

1.2 Prepare to introduce yourself to some other members of the class. Write down which topic areas you will talk about, and in which order.

1.3 Introduce yourself to other members of your group and find out about them. Remember to make a note of their names. Use **Repair expressions** (see the Language Help section page 139), as appropriate, to prevent communication from breaking down.

Step 3: Discussion and reporting back

1.4 Form a group and discuss the following statements[1] for ten minutes. Do not spend longer than two minutes on any one statement. Make sure that a different member of the group writes down the main points for each statement.

    a) I want to speak English with a perfect native-speaker accent.
    b) I want to speak English without a single grammatical mistake.
    c) I must enlarge my vocabulary in order to improve my spoken English.
    d) I feel as though I am a different person when I speak English.
    e) If I read English, my spoken English will benefit as well.
    f) The best way to improve my spoken English is to speak, as often as possible, to as many different people as possible.
    g) I don't speak as much as I would like to because I'm afraid of making mistakes.
    h) I don't like working in groups because I may learn incorrect English from my classmates.

1.5 Report back to the rest of the class on the most interesting or controversial point(s) that came out of your discussion.

Step 4: Before the next session

1.6 Read the Learner Questionnaire on pages 107-9. Complete Part 1.

SESSION 2

Step 1: Preparation

2.1 Look at the diagram indicated by your teacher. Prepare to summarise the information conveyed by the diagram.

Step 2: Information exchange and discussion

2.2 Form a pair with someone who looked at a different diagram in 2.1. Without looking at your partner's diagram at all, summarise for him/her the information

[1] This exercise is adapted from M.Geddes and G. Sturtridge, *Advanced Conversation*, Macmillan, 1991.

conveyed by your diagram. When it is your partner's turn to summarise, note down the main points you find out about his/her diagram.

2.3 What do you find is the single, most interesting point to emerge from the diagrams? Find out whether you and your partner agree on this.

 Step 3: Review

2.4 Think back to how you and your partner carried out the information-exchange task in 2.2 above. Answer the following questions:
1) Did you succeed in exchanging the relevant information?
2) What could you or your partner have done to make the exchange more efficient?

2.5 Read through the checklist of strategies for exchanging information efficiently, and answer these questions:
1) Which of the strategies did you and your partner use in 2.2?
2) Which of the other strategies might have enabled you to exchange information more efficiently?

STRATEGIES FOR EXCHANGING INFORMATION EFFICIENTLY

- **Decide procedure**
  Decide with your partner on a suitable procedure for exchanging the information.

- **Frame information**
  Frame the information as a whole first, before going into detail.

- **Check on partner's understanding**
  Check that your partner has understood your point correctly.

- **Paraphrase**
  If your partner seems not to understand a particular word/phrase, paraphrase it. (Don't just go on repeating it!)

- **Check on your understanding**
  If you're not sure about a particular point made by your partner, check whether you have understood it correctly.

- **Ask clear questions**
  If you don't understand a particular point made by your partner, ask for clarification.
  If you ask a question, make the subject/purpose of it clear to your partner.

Step 4: Exchange and discussion

2.6 Form a group and discuss your answers to the following questions from the Learner Questionnaire (pages 107-9):

1) How do you feel about communicating orally in English?
2) Do you think it will be important during your academic course to be able to communicate orally? What sort of oral activities or tasks will you be expected to carry out in your department?

SESSION 3

Step 1: Preparing to listen

3.1 You intend to study at an English-medium college or university in the near future. Discuss the following questions:

1) Have you got a clear idea of what your intended course will be like?
2) Do you expect the style of teaching and learning to be similar to that on previous courses you have done?

3.2 You are going to listen to a British university tutor talk about the course he/she supervises and about his/her experience with international students. What questions are you interested in hearing him/her answer?

Step 2: Listening and checking

3.3 Look through the questions on the worksheet on page 5. Listen to the recording once and take notes of the tutor's comments without stopping the tape.

3.4 Confer with the other members of your group about the answers for the worksheet. Play the recording a second time, stopping and rewinding as necessary. Complete the appropriate column of the worksheet.

Step 3: Information exchange and discussion

3.5 Pair up with someone who listened to the other recording. Exchange information to complete the worksheet.

3.6 Discuss the following questions about the two courses:

1) Does the style of teaching/learning seem to be similar in the two cases?
2) In what ways is it different from previous courses you and your partner have been on?
3) The tutors refer to various types of oral communication task. Which type sounds most challenging to you?

	TEXT 1	TEXT 2
1. What is the name of the person interviewed?		
2. Which course/department is he/she involved in?		
3. How many international students are there?		
4. Does he/she find that the international students have a lot of language problems?		

5. For what purpose do students need to be able to communicate well orally?

TEXT 1	TEXT 2
a)	a)
b)	b)
c)	c)
d)	d)
e)	e)

6. What advice does he/she give international students?

TEXT 1	TEXT 2
a)	a)
	b)
	c)

Step 4: Language review

3.7 Re-read **Repair expressions** in the Language Help section on page 139. Add any useful language you have met in this unit.

3.8 Look at the vocabulary map which has been started on page 7. With a partner, think back over the activities you have done in this unit and extend the map by adding any useful words that you have come across related to the topic of Academic Study. Use a dictionary if necessary.

Step 5: Before the next session

3.9 Complete Part 2 of the Learner Questionnaire (page 109). Your teacher may want to discuss your answers with you.

LEARNER DIARY ONE

Previous experience

Read the following questions and make some notes in answer to the ones that most interest you. These notes are primarily for your own attention, but you may find it helpful to discuss them with your teacher. For more information about keeping a Learner Diary see page 110.

1. How much speaking in and listening to English have you done in the last five years?

2. What kind of topics did you listen to/talk about?

3. Who did you listen/talk to in English?

4. To what extent has this experience prepared you for academic study in English?

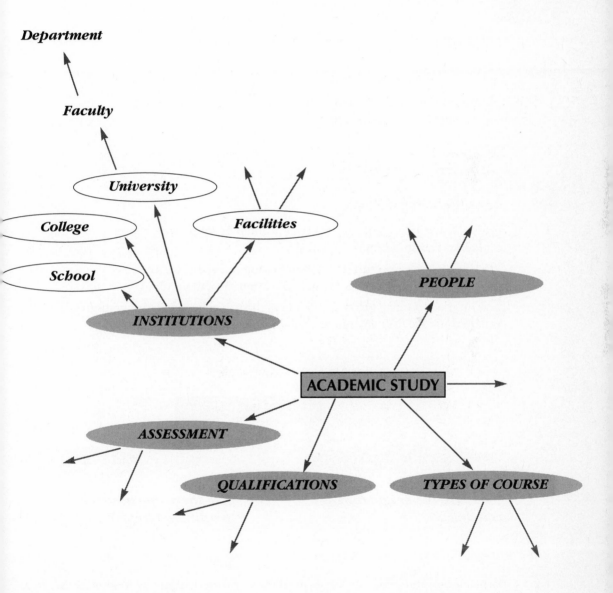

Department

Faculty

University

College

Facilities

School

INSTITUTIONS

PEOPLE

ACADEMIC STUDY

ASSESSMENT

QUALIFICATIONS

TYPES OF COURSE

UNIT

1

COUNTRIES

SKILLS FOCUS: Preparing a presentation

SESSION 1

Step 1: Exploring the topic

1.1   Imagine that a fellow student, who is of a different nationality[1] from you, is going to speak to you about his/her country:

- What would you be interested in finding out about the country?
- What questions would you like to ask him/her about it?

Develop the ideas map below by adding as many headings and/or questions as you can think of. Use any symbols or abbreviations you think appropriate.

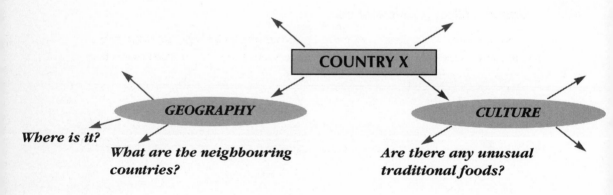

COUNTRY X

GEOGRAPHY

Where is it?

What are the neighbouring countries?

CULTURE

Are there any unusual traditional foods?

1.2   Form a group and pool your ideas. Add to your own map any interesting ideas that you had not thought of previously.

   [1]If you and your classmates are all from the **same** country, imagine that this fellow student is going to speak about his/her district.

Step 2: Preparing to collect information

1.3 In the same group, use the ideas in your maps to make a list of questions which will form the basis of an interview with someone about their country. Organise your questions under sub-headings of different topic areas. Your teacher will collect your group's list at the end of the lesson.

Step 3: Language focus

1.4 Your teacher is going to give a short presentation about his/her country or district. Afterwards you may want to ask him/her a question about something you did not understand or something you would like to hear more about. Look now at **Asking questions after a presentation** in the Language Help section on page 127 and practise the expressions. Choose at least one expression to use at the end of your teacher's presentation.

1.5 As you listen to your teacher, take notes of the main points he/she makes about his/her country. Then, following the presentation, use the expression(s) you have chosen to ask about anything you did not understand or would like to hear more about.

Step 4: Extending your ideas map

1.6 If your teacher's presentation contained any topic areas or questions that you had not included in your map, add them to it.

SESSION 2

Step 1: Collecting information

2.1 Find out from your teacher whether you are going to be the informant or one of the researchers in this activity, and then carry out the relevant instructions below.

INSTRUCTIONS FOR THE INFORMANT

Stage 1 Think about the language that you are likely to need when answering questions about your country. Consult a dictionary to make sure that you are pronouncing and stressing the key words correctly. Ask your teacher if necessary.

Stage 2 Co-operate with the researchers. Answer their questions as clearly and accurately as you can.

> ### INSTRUCTIONS FOR THE RESEARCHERS
>
> **Stage 1** Your teacher will give you a copy of the class question list, and tell you which section of it you are to be responsible for. Practise saying the questions in that section, until you are able to do so accurately and fluently without reading from the list. If you think of other relevant questions add them to your section of the list.
>
> **Stage 2** You have a maximum of five minutes to collect information from the informant in answer to the questions in your section of the question list. If you need more information than the informant gives you at first, ask follow-up questions. Take notes of the main points made by the informant.

Step 2: Drafting an outline

2.2   In your group, look through all the information that you have collected. Discuss the following questions and then draft an outline of your presentation about your informant's country:

NB (i) You will have only six minutes to give the presentation.
    (ii) The informant will not be allowed to contribute during the presentation.

1) How many major points can an audience take in during a six-minute presentation?
2) What are the three or four most important points for you to get across to your audience?
3) What is the best order to present the points in?
4) What would be an effective opening?
5) How will you conclude?
6) Is the overall structure clear and logical?

Step 3: Discussion – using aids

2.3   Discuss the following:

1) For what reason(s) would you use a visual aid when giving a presentation?
2) Look at the two display-outlines indicated by your teacher. Which of them would have been more effective in helping the audience to recognise the main sections of the presentation? Why?
3) What are the dos and don'ts to remember when producing a display-outline? Make a note of the most important ones in the table opposite.

DO	DON'T
1.	1.
2.	2.
3.	3.

    4) For what purpose would you use a handout when giving a presentation?

Step 4: Drafting aids

2.4   Discuss the following questions:

    1) What headings will you use in your display-outline to guide the audience through the presentation?

    2) What other visual aids would be useful, if any?

    3) Would a handout be helpful? If so, containing what kind of information?

    4) What essential information do you need for your own use on a prompt-sheet or prompt-cards?

2.5   Draft the aids that you decided upon in 2.4.

Step 5: Before the next class

2.6   Decide with your teacher which group member(s) will give the presentation next time.

2.7   Check that:

    1) your poster/OHT is neat and easily legible when shown on the board/screen.

    2) you are able to operate the projector (if you are working with OHTs).

SESSION 3

Step 1: Discussion

3.1   Think back over talks, lectures or presentations (in any language) that you yourself have attended, and discuss the following question:

    • What makes some presentations more successful than others?

Step 2: Giving a presentation

3.2   Group 1 now gives its presentation to the rest of the class. Members of the other groups listen and take notes. At the end of the presentation Group 1's speaker invites questions from the audience; other members of Group 1 should be ready to answer these questions.

Step 3: Preparing feedback

3.3   Read through **Assessing Presentations: Checklist 1** on page 112 and decide with other members of your group how you should complete it in order to give appropriate feedback to Group 1 on their presentation. Each group member (except members of Group 1) should complete the checklist with the feedback from his/her group, and should be ready to explain that feedback to members of Group 1.

Step 4: Repeat for other groups

3.4   Repeat steps 3.2 and 3.3 for each of the other groups in the class.

Step 5: Exchanging feedback

3.5   Sit with people from different groups. Exchange the completed checklists and read through the feedback that the other groups have offered your group. Ask for explanations if you want (e.g. 'You didn't think our OHTs were clear; in what way were they unclear?').

3.6   Decide as a class, with your teacher, which group was the best for each of the criteria in Checklist 1.

Step 6: Language review

3.7   Re-read **Asking questions after a presentation** in the Language Help section on page 127. Add any useful language you have met in this unit.

3.8   Look at the vocabulary map which has been started on page 14. With a partner, think back over the activities you have done in this unit and extend the map by adding any useful words that you have come across related to the topic of Countries. Use a dictionary if necessary.

Step 7: Before the next session

3.9   Listen to the recording of your group's presentation and look at the comments made on it by your teacher.

3.10 Read through the model for preparing a presentation on page 114 and the list of prompt questions that follow. Note down anything you do not understand, so that you can ask about it in class next time.

LEARNER DIARY TWO
....

Making a presentation

1. Describe at least one strength and one weakness of your presentations in English.

2. The model on page 114 identifies a number of the steps you may go through in preparing a presentation. Is your own procedure for preparing a presentation (in any language) similar to this model? Which steps do you regard as particularly important or difficult?

3. Next time you give a presentation in English, which aspect (e.g. timing, clear voice, clear organisation) are you going to concentrate on improving?

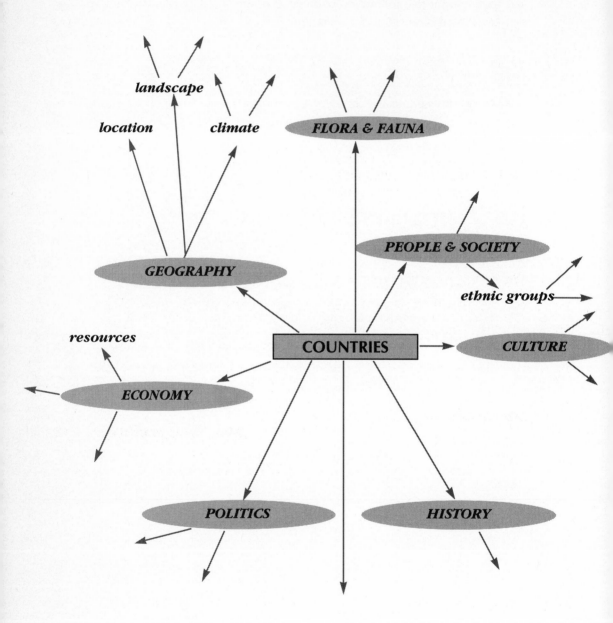

UNIT 2

THE HOME

SESSION 1

Step 1: Warm-up/Discussion

1.1 In pairs, tell each other about the home(s) you have lived in up to now.

Step 2: Collecting information

1.2 Complete the ideas map below, adding your own questions about the home.

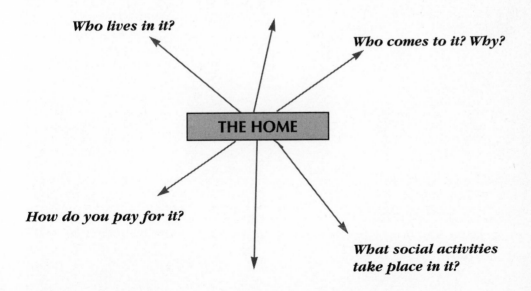

Who lives in it?

Who comes to it? Why?

THE HOME

How do you pay for it?

What social activities take place in it?

Questionnaire: The Home in Britain and ....

QUESTION	IN BRITAIN	IN MY COUNTRY/DISTRICT
1. Who lives in the typical home?		
2. How do you pay for it?		
3. Who comes to it? Why?		
4. What social activities take place in it?		
5.		
6.		

1.3 Add your two questions (as 5 and 6) to the questionnaire.

1.4 Find out from your teacher the answers to the questions about the home in Britain. Fill in the middle column of the table with this information.

1.5 Complete the right-hand column in the table with notes on the home in your own country.[1]

Step 3: Preparing for your audience

1.6 You are going to prepare a two-minute talk on the home in your country or district using some of the information from 1.5. Your audience will be your classmates. Before you prepare your talk, note down your answers to the following questions:

  1) What (if anything) will a classmate know about the home in your country/ district?

  2) What will a classmate not know about the home in your country/district?

  3) What will a classmate find interesting about the home in your country/ district?

Then, focus your talk on things you noted down for 2) and/or 3).

SESSION 2

Step 1: Giving short talks

2.1 Sit in pairs. One person in each pair will give his/her two-minute talk on the home in his/her country or district.

2.2 From time to time, the teacher will stop the talks and ask the listeners to carry out one of the following instructions:

- recap the speaker's last point
- contradict the speaker's last point
- summarise what the speaker has said so far
- ask for more information about one of the speaker's points
- predict the speaker's next point.

2.3 Change roles with your partner, with the listener giving his/her talk.

2.4 Change partners and repeat twice.

2.5 At the end of the class, select two students to give an expanded version of their talk (a five-minute presentation) to the whole group next lesson.

2.6 Note down two things the two students should remember about their audience as they prepare their presentations.

---

[1]If you and your classmates are from the **same** country, refer to your district (either within your country or within your town) throughout this unit, instead of country.

Step 2: Before the next session

2.7 If you are studying in Britain, complete as much as you can of the quiz below by asking people and/or looking at houses. If you are not studying in Britain, answer quiz question 6 only.

2.8 What typical items from the home in your country (eating utensils, for example) would you take with you if you were going to live abroad? If possible, find one or two of these items (or pictures of them) to bring to the next class. (Read 3.8 on pages 19-20.)

2.9 The two students selected in 2.5 should prepare their five-minute presentations, remembering the points raised in 1.6 and 2.6.

Quiz: The Home in Britain

1. Find the names of two houses.

2. What is an allotment?

3. Find three different kinds of home on your route to class from where you are staying.

4. Find three different things people can have in their garden (apart from plants!).

5. Complete the following English proverbs:

   a) "An Englishman's home ...."

   b) "Home is where ...."

   c) "..., home's best."

6. Do you have any proverbs about the home in your country? What are they, translated into English?

SESSION 3

Step 1: Checking the quiz

3.1 Go over the answers to the quiz from Session 2.

Step 2: Giving presentations

3.2 One of the students selected in 2.5 gives his/her presentation to the class and then answers any questions that arise.

3.3 The listeners answer the audience feedback questions after the presentation.

Audience Feedback

1. How much of the information in the presentation was new to you?

   ALL   MOST   SOME   A BIT   NONE

2. Did the speaker help you follow the main points?

   YES   A LITTLE   NO

3. How interesting was the presentation?

   VERY / QUITE / NOT interesting

   Why?

3.4 Repeat for the second speaker.

3.5 The two speakers receive feedback on their presentations.

3.6 List advice about the audience that you would give someone doing their first presentation.

Step 3: Describing and explaining

3.7 Look at **Describing an object** in the Language Help section on page 131 and then do the following practice exercises:

    1) Describe the following items using these expressions:
        a pencil
        a bicycle
        a computer

    2) Think of a common object. Describe this object to your partner without naming it until he/she guesses what it is.

3.8 Choose three household items from your own country that you would take with you to set up home abroad. Select items because you think they are typical/unusual/unavailable abroad/any other reason you like! If you have brought any objects or pictures to class as a result of 2.8, you can include these items in your list.

3.9 Prepare notes and/or diagrams to use in describing your items to other students. You will also need to explain why you have chosen them.

3.10 In groups of four or five, describe and explain your items. Each person has a *maximum of five minutes*.

3.11 Each person in the group must select one item from another person's list to present to the whole class.

3.12 Each person then has *one minute* to present to the whole class the chosen item from the list of a fellow group member, explaining why he/she chose it.

Step 4: Language review

3.13 Re-read **Describing an object** in the Language Help section on page 131. Add any useful language you have met in this unit.

3.14 Look at the vocabulary map which has been started on page 21. With a partner, think back over the activities you have done in this unit and extend the map by adding any useful words that you have come across related to the topic of The Home. Use a dictionary if necessary.

Step 5: Before the next session

3.15 Answer questions about Education in your own country by completing the relevant part of the questionnaire (Column B) in Unit 3 on page 23.

LEARNER DIARY THREE

Expanding your vocabulary

1. In what areas do you need to expand your vocabulary?

2. What can/do you do to expand your vocabulary?

3. What is the best way for you to keep a record of new vocabulary? How do you feel about the vocabulary maps you have produced so far in this course?

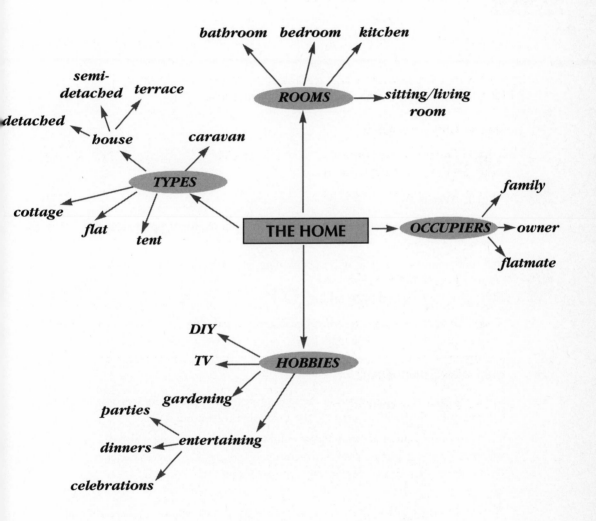

UNIT

3 EDUCATION

SKILLS FOCUS: Looking for ideas to shape your talk

SESSION 1

Step 1: Warm-up

1.1 Think about your experience of education. Note down three aspects of it that you have liked and three that you have not liked.

1.2 Tell your partner about these aspects, explaining why you did or did not like them.

Step 2: Listening and note taking

1.3 Take notes as you listen to a recorded introductory talk on the English education system. You will need to refer to these notes later in order to answer some questions on the subject.

Step 3: Information transfer

1.4 Which (if any) of the questions in the questionnaire on page 23 are you able to answer with regard to England? Complete the first column (column A).

1.5 If you and your partner are from *different* countries, ask him/her questions to obtain information about his/her country to complete column C. Answer his/her questions on your country using notes you have made in column B.

or

If you and your partner are from the *same* country, discuss your answers in column B and write the main differences between England and your country in column C.

Questionnaire: Education in England, ... and ....

	A) In England	B) In my country	C) In another country
1. Between which ages is education compulsory?			
2. Are schools free or fee-paying?			
3. What are the stages and ages of pupils in the school system?			
4. Do you have a national curriculum?			
5. What qualifications can pupils get at school?			
6. How do pupils get into university?			
7. How long is the average undergraduate course?			

SESSION 2

Step 1: Language focus

2.1 Look at the tapescript of the talk on the English education system on page 89. Was the talk easy to follow? Why? How did the speaker help the listener to follow what she was saying?

2.2 Highlight or underline the words in the talk that helped in this way.

Step 2: Short presentations

2.3 In groups of three or four, collect a set of expression cards from the teacher. Look through the expressions and try to organise them into sets according to their function.

2.4 Give each set of expressions a label. For example, *Asking for clarification* or *Indicating the start of a new section*.

2.5 Look at pages 126 **(Asking for clarification)** and 141 **(Signpost expressions)** in the Language Help section to check your classification.

2.6 Divide the sets into 'speaker expressions' and 'audience expressions'.

2.7 Collect a set of topic cards from the teacher, placing them face down in a pile on your table.

2.8 Each person must select one topic card and spend two minutes noting down things to say on this topic, considering the following questions:

1) What conclusions will your talk lead to?
2) What main points will you mention?

EXAMPLE TOPIC: Computers

1. useful tool, but must not replace human responsibility/contact
2. save time, efficient, getting cheaper so more people have access <u>but</u> can crash/get viruses →chaos; 'have-nots' disadvantaged further; discourage person-to-person communication.

2.9 Choose one member of your group to be the first speaker. He/she must select three 'speaker-expression' cards at random, and then speak for 90 seconds on the topic selected, using all three of the expressions on the cards.

The other members of the group listen and prepare to ask a question on the topic at the end of the talk, each using one of the audience-expressions cards. Appoint one of the listeners as the timekeeper; he/she should tell the speaker clearly when one minute has passed and then, after 90 seconds, ask the speaker to stop immediately and answer questions from the group.

2.10 Repeat the procedure described in 2.8 with a different speaker and timekeeper, until each member of your group has been the speaker.

Step 3: Before the next session

2.11 If you are in a class with students from *different* countries, prepare a five-minute presentation on the strengths and weaknesses of the education system in your country.

or

If you are in a class with students from the *same* country as yourself, prepare a five-minute presentation on issues for the future for your country's education system.

REMEMBER THE FOLLOWING:

1. Before you start, note down answers to the questions in 2.8 to help you establish a focus for your presentation.

2. Prepare notes for your presentation that will help you explain your main, overall point and your line of argument.

3. Practise by yourself/with a friend and time yourself to make sure you can keep to five minutes.

4. It will be especially important to use signpost expressions to make the organisation of information clear to your audience, as you will not be able to use OHTs or a blackboard.

Do not forget to bring your notes for this presentation to the next session.

SESSION 3

Step 1: Presentations

3.1 In groups of four, appoint a timekeeper.

3.2 Give your five-minute prepared presentations in turn. The listeners take notes.

3.3 After each presentation, compare the listeners' notes with the speaker's notes and consider the following questions:

1. Did the audience manage to recognise and note down
   a) the main, overall point?
   b) the line of argument?
   c) the conclusion?
2. Did the speaker make adequate and appropriate use of signpost expressions to help the audience follow his/her talk?

3.4 Note down your answers to the following question:

In a presentation, how can a speaker help the audience identify:
a) the main point?
b) the line of argument?
c) the conclusion?

Step 2: Group discussion and mini-presentation

3.5 Decide in your group on the five most important features of the ideal education. Choose from the list on page 27 and add other features or principles of your own if you like.

3.6 Rank the five features in order of importance.

3.7 Agree (if you can!) on your group's main, overall point about education. If you cannot agree, note down the main areas of difference.

3.8 Prepare to explain and justify your main point (or differences) about education and your selection of five features to the whole class, using visual aids (e.g. OHTs, diagrams on the blackboard, posters) as appropriate.

3.9 Each group presents to the class.

Step 3: Language review

3.10 Re-read **Signpost expressions** in the Language Help section on page 141. Add any useful language you have met in this unit.

3.11 With a partner, think back over the activities you have done in this unit and make a vocabulary map, adding any useful words that you have come across related to the topic of Education. Use a dictionary if necessary.

Step 4: Before the next session

3.12 Read **Reviewing Discussion: Checklist 3** on page 118 and answer 'Part 1 The Individual' with reference to the discussion in Step 2.

LEARNER DIARY FOUR

Pronunciation

1. What are the strengths and weaknesses of your pronunciation in English? Think about individual sounds, combinations of sounds, stress and intonation.

2. How do you check that your pronunciation is correct?

3. What can you do to improve upon/compensate for your weaknesses?

THE IDEAL EDUCATION

Education at school should .....

1. ... instill in children an ethical code to apply in later life.

2. ... teach religion.

3. ... be co-educational.

4. ... discipline children so that they respect and obey their elders.

5. ... train children so that they can get a job when they leave school.

6. ... require all children to wear a uniform.

7. ... teach children to express themselves.

8. ... prepare children for higher education.

9. ... occupy children for at least eight hours a day.

10. ... not be free of charge – you don't get anything valuable for nothing.

11. ... include compulsory team sports.

12. ... have no more than five children in a class.

13. ... be demanding and should stretch children in order to prepare them for the competitive nature of adult life in the modern world.

14. ... be prepared to employ corporal punishment to deal with disruptive behaviour.

15. ....

16. ....

17. ....

18. ....

UNIT 4

THE FAMILY

SKILLS FOCUS: Collecting information

SESSION 1

Step 1: Discussion

1.1 Form groups of four or five; one of you will observe and the rest will discuss the following topic: *The family does more harm than good.*
Write down at least two ideas that you would like to contribute to the discussion.

1.2 Discuss the topic, with the observer present but not participating.

Step 2: Feedback on group dynamics

1.3 As a group, discuss questions 11 and 12 in Part 2 of **Reviewing Discussion: Checklist 3** on page 118.

1.4 Discuss the observer's diagram and what it shows about a) individual contributions and b) group dynamics (how members of a group interact).

1.5 Discuss questions 13 and 14 in Part 2 of **Reviewing Discussion: Checklist 3**.

1.6 List below three ways in which you can improve your own contribution to discussion, and three things the group could do in their next discussion to make it more effective.

My contribution	The group
1.	1.
2.	2.
3.	3.

1.7 What are the signs/characteristics of successful group dynamics? Add to your table any useful suggestions from other groups.

Step 3: Collecting information on British families

1.8 What (if anything) do you know about the family in Britain? Make a list under the following headings:

1) Things I **know** for certain (e.g. There are families in Britain.).
2) Things I think I know but I am **not sure** about (e.g. The divorce rate is very high.).
3) Things I would **like to know** (e.g. the number of children in the average family).

1.9 Read *one* of the two texts about families in Britain, either A on page 68 or B on page 72. Your teacher will tell you which.

1.10 Highlight the main points in this text. You can do this by underlining or using a highlighter pen. Make sure that you bring your highlighted text to class for use in Session 2.

Session 2

Step 1: Preparing for a presentation

2.1 Work with other people who read the *same* family text as you in Session 1 above. Look at the list you made for 1.8. Is there any information in your text that can confirm points made under 1) or 2) or that provides information needed for 3)? If so, make a note of this information.

2.2 Decide on the headings or brief outline that you would use in giving a short presentation (maximum: five minutes) of the main points in the text.

2.3 Make notes from the text to use in giving your presentation. Remember to include the information you found in 2.1.

2.4 Prepare one or more OHTs or posters to use in the presentation.

2.5 Decide together which member of your group will give the presentation next time. He/she should practise in front of the group with the notes and the OHTs/posters, plus a timekeeper. Decide what to do if the presentation is too long (e.g. cut out some information; spend less time on an OHT/poster).

Step 2: Before the next session

2.6 The *presenters* chosen in 2.5 must rehearse their presentations again, making sure they can present well and keep to the time limit.

2.7 If you are in a class with students from *different* countries, *all other class members* (not the presenters in 2.5) must prepare a short talk (maximum: four minutes) about families in their own country. Use the same headings as your group decided on in 2.2 above. You can make comparisons with British families if you like. You are not expected to have lots of statistics at your fingertips, just give a general idea. Look in the Language Help section at **Comparison and contrast** (page 129) and **Describing trends** (page 132) for some useful expressions.

or

If you are in a class with students from the *same* country as yourself, your teacher will suggest a topic to you.

Do not forget to bring your notes for this short talk to the next session.

SESSION 3

Step 1: Presentation (based on Text A)

3.1   The person chosen to present the main points from Text A now does so to the whole class (five minutes maximum).

- Everyone who worked on **Text A** listens to check that all the main points are accurately reported.
- Everyone who worked on **Text B** takes notes on the information from Text A.

Step 2: Following the presentation

3.2   Any corrections can be made to the content by other people who worked on Text A.

3.3   People who worked on Text B can ask the presenter to clarify anything they were unsure of in the presentation.

3.4   Everyone, including the presenter, now spends three minutes answering the questions on **Assessing Presentations: Checklist for Unit 4** on page 32.

Step 3: Second presentation (based on Text B)

3.5   Repeat Steps 1 and 2, but this time the presentation is about Text B.

Step 4: Feedback

3.6   Hand the answers from 3.4 to the presenters.

3.7   *Presenters:* read through the answers and note down three improvements that you will make in your next presentation. *The rest of the class:* divide into groups and decide on two or three strengths of each presentation (look at the checklist for ideas if you want to).

3.8   The groups report back on the presentations' strengths.

3.9   The presenters explain to the class the improvements they intend to make next time.

Step 5: Presentations (about the topic prepared for in 2.7)

3.10 The class redivides into two groups, with an equal number of Text A and Text B people in each group.

3.11 Each person in turn, except the two who presented on Texts A and B in 3.1 above, now talks to the group about the family in his/her own country or another topic from 2.7. Appoint a timekeeper to ensure that the time limit of four minutes per person is kept to. The timekeeper must indicate after three minutes and stop the speaker after four minutes.

3.12 Select one person in each group to repeat his/her presentation to the whole class. Decide together on one improvement that he/she should try to make on this second attempt.

3.13 The two people chosen in 3.12 give their presentations.

3.14 If you are in the audience, try to ask a question after one of these two presentations.

Step 6: Language review

3.15 Re-read **Comparison and contrast** on page 129 and **Describing trends** on page 132. Add any useful language you have met in this unit.

3.16 With a partner, think back over the activities you have done in this unit and make a vocabulary map adding any useful words that you have come across related to the topic of The Family. Use a dictionary if necessary.

LEARNER DIARY FIVE

Taking part in a discussion

1. How successfully do you think you contributed to class discussions this week?

2. What are your strengths and weaknesses in discussion in English?

3. How useful do you find the Reviewing Discussion Checklist on page 118?

4. What do you intend to practise in next week's discussion activities?

ASSESSING PRESENTATIONS: CHECKLIST FOR UNIT 4

1. Was the presentation easy to follow?	no / quite / yes
2. Did the OHT clearly show:	
a) the main headings?	no / yes
b) any difficult vocabulary?	no / yes
c) any difficult figures?	no / yes
3. Did the speaker maintain sufficient eye-contact with the audience?	no / yes
4. Comment on the speaker's voice:	
a) speed	too fast / too slow / about right
b) volume	too quiet / about right
c) pitch variation	monotonous / expressive
5. TO BE ANSWERED BY THE PEOPLE WHO READ THE SAME TEXT	
a) Was the information factually correct?	no / some / yes
b) Was the most important information presented?	no / some / yes
6. TO BE ANSWERED BY THE PEOPLE WHO READ THE OTHER TEXT	
a) Could you understand the information?	all / most / some / little
b) Could you identify the main points?	all / most / some / few

7. What could the speaker do to improve the presentation next time?

UNIT 5

THE MEDIA

SESSION 1

Step 1: Warm-up

1.1 We make use of a great variety of information and entertainment media today. If you could use only one of the following over the next year, which one would you choose? Why?

newspapers   *radio*   *personal computer linked to the Internet*
audio-cassette and compact disc player   *television*
personal stereo   *video-cassette player*

Step 2: Vocabulary - different kinds of programme

1.2 **Matching definitions**
In the left-hand column below are eight words commonly used for kinds of TV or radio programme. Match each word with the appropriate definition in the right-hand column.

soap opera	1. Comedy of character and situation, involving the same characters in each episode.
quiz show	2. An informative, in-depth examination of a fairly serious topic.
game show	3. Adaptation of a major work of literature.
chat show	4. Long-running drama of the day-to-day experience of a community of characters.
sitcom	5. A programme in which the public takes part by phoning in with comments.
documentary	6. A programme in which a presenter asks a celebrity to talk about him/herself.
classic drama	7. A programme in which contestants take part in various games to win prizes.
phone-in	8. A programme in which contestants try to score points by answering questions correctly.

1.3   Discussion
- Which kind of programme do you watch most often in your own country?
- Which kind do you least enjoy?
- Which kinds have you seen examples of on British television, if any?

Think of a particular programme that you especially enjoyed or disliked in the last year or so. Briefly describe the programme and explain your reaction to it.

Step 3: Describing charts

1.4   Transferring information from a chart
Your teacher will indicate which chart you will look at. Look at either Chart 1 (**TV programmes produced by the BBC: programme hours by category**) or Chart 2 (**TV programmes produced by the BBC: production cost by category**). Discuss questions 1 to 5 below the chart with a partner who looked at the same chart, and then note down your answers.

1.5   Exchanging information
Form a pair with someone who looked at a different chart from you in 1.4. Ask your partner the questions 6 to 10 below your chart and note down his/her answers. When it is your turn to answer questions, try to do so by looking at your chart rather than at your notes.

1.6   Language practice
To practise the correct word order and pronunciation, take it in turns with your partner to convert each short answer (questions 1-4 and 6-9) into a complete statement.

For example:

> **Q** Which is the smallest category in terms of cost?
> **A** Sport.
> → Sport is the smallest category in terms of cost.
> *or* The smallest category in terms of cost is sport.
> *or* In terms of cost, the smallest category is sport.

1.7   Discussion
Using the information from both charts, discuss the following questions:
1) Which kind of programme is the most expensive to produce in terms of cost per hour?
2) Which is the least expensive in terms of cost per hour?
3) Can you suggest possible reasons for these being the most/least expensive?

1.8   Consolidation
Look at Chart 3 (**TV programmes produced by the BBC: production cost per hour**). Note down words to fill the gaps in the extract below from a talk about producing television programmes. Each gap requires a single word or phrase.

'... Production costs vary widely from one category of programme to another. This chart illustrates that point very clearly. As you can see, in terms of cost per hour (1__) is by far the most expensive category of programme to produce. It is more than (2 __) as expensive as Entertainment, and nearly twelve times as expensive as (3 __) at the other end of the scale. (4__) programmes, which arguably contribute more to the BBC's reputation than any other category, are relatively cheap to produce, at only £78,000 per hour, and may therefore represent the best value of all the categories .... '

SESSION 2

Step 1: Anticipation questions

2.1   You are going to listen to a BBC editor talk about the BBC – its funding, its audience, its relationship with government, etc. Write down three questions that you would like him to answer.

2.2   Pool your questions with a fellow student.

2.3   As a class, draw up a list of eight questions.

Step 2: Listening

2.4   Listen to either Text 1 or Text 2, and take notes of the main points made by the speaker.

Step 3: Preparation - giving an overview

2.5   With a partner who listened to the *same* text, decide which headings you will use to organise a summary of that text for someone who has not heard it.

As well as helping you to remember what you intend to say and in what order, these headings also enable you to start your talk in a way that is helpful to the audience, by giving them an overview to guide their listening. For example, 'The speaker in Text 1 covered three main areas: the origins of the United Nations Organisation, its funding arrangements, and its main achievements. On the first of these, the origins of the UN, he explained that ...'

Step 4: Exchanging information

2.6   Form a pair with someone who listened to a *different* text from you in 2.4. Take it in turns to summarise the text you listened to. Start your summary with an overview of the headings you decided on in 2.5. When your partner summarises his/her text, take notes.

Step 5: Review

2.7 With your partner's help, answer the following questions:

- Did your overview help your partner to follow your summary?
- Did your overview help you to present the summary?
- How could your overview have been improved?

2.8 Look back at the list of anticipation questions (from 2.3) and see how many of them you are now able to answer from one or other of the texts.

Step 6: Before the next session

2.9 Prepare to tell your classmates about the media in your country.[1] Your talk should last for five to six minutes. The following prompt questions from the list on page 115 may help you to prepare.

Generating ideas

- What is interesting about the topic?
- What would the audience like to find out about the topic?
- What about the topic would surprise the audience?

Drafting outline and aids

- What are the three or four most important points for you to get across to your audience?
- What headings will you use in your overview to guide the audience?

SESSION 3

Step 1: Presentation

3.1 Form a group. Each person has a maximum of six minutes for their presentation, starting with an overview of what he/she is going to say.

Step 2: Review

3.2 Decide which country's media you now know most about. What made that speaker's talk successful? How did he/she help you to follow the talk?

Step 3: Preparation

3.3 Individually, prepare your thoughts for a discussion of the following topic: *The power of*

---

[1]If you and your classmates are all from the same country, prepare to talk about a particular aspect of the media in your country – e.g. the press, radio, TV, international media, etc.

the media in today's world: a force for good? Write down at least two points that you would like to contribute to the discussion.

Step 4: Language focus

3.4 Read through **Asking for clarification** in the Language Help section on page 126. Choose two expressions to use when you need clarification in the discussion that follows.

Step 5: Discussion and reporting back

3.5 Form a group to conduct the discussion. Appoint a secretary to note down the main points of your group's answer. During the discussion, try to contribute the two points that you noted down in 3.3, and use the expressions to ask for clarification when necessary.

3.6 One member of each group reports to the class on the main points in his/her group's discussion. Listen to find out whether other groups broadly agree or disagree with you.

Step 6: Language review

3.7 Re-read **Asking for clarification** in the Language Help section on page 126. Add any useful language you have met in this unit.

3.8 With a partner, think back over the activities you have done in this unit and draw a map, adding any useful words that you have come across related to the topic of The Media. Use a dictionary if necessary.

LEARNER DIARY SIX

Taking stock

1. In the Foundation Unit Learner Questionnaire (page 107) you were asked what in particular you would concentrate on improving in the first half of the course. Have you succeeded in making that improvement?

2. What in particular are you going to concentrate on improving in the second half of the course?

3. What practical steps are you going to take in the next week in order to begin this improvement?

UNIT 6 HEALTH

SKILLS FOCUS: Preparing a group presentation

SESSION 1

Step 1: Extending vocabulary

1.1 Write down as many words related to Health as you can think of in 60 seconds.

1.2 In a small group, make a Health vocabulary map on an OHT or poster, containing some/all of the words you have thought of.

Step 2: Collecting information

1.3 Complete both parts of the Health questionnaire on pages 41 and 42 by noting down your answers for Part A on one piece of paper and for Part B on another piece.

1.4 Divide into two groups (A and B) to process the questionnaire data. Group A collects the answers to Part A of the questionnaire to work on, Group B does the same for the answers to Part B. Each group will have to make a presentation based on the questionnaire data it has.

1.5 In your group:
   1) decide on a procedure for processing the data
   2) process it
   3) prepare the presentation.

SESSION 2

Step 1: Language focus

2.1 Look at **Expressing proportion** in the Language Help section (on page 136).

Step 2: Processing questionnaire data

2.2   In Groups A and B, discuss:

> 1) your questionnaire results
> 2) how to present them to the whole class.

Step 3: Preparing the group presentation

2.3   You will have a maximum of 12 minutes to give the presentation of your results and at least three people must be involved in giving it. Therefore your group must now:

---

1. **Organise your content**
   Decide:
   - what information to include (remember the time limit; focus on points that are interesting)
   - the best order in which to present the information
   - what information is best conveyed visually
   - how to convey it visually (e.g. table/chart/graph? on OHT/poster/whiteboard?)

2. **Prepare for the presentation**
   - decide on the different parts of the presentation
   - decide who will present which part
   - think of an effective opening and conclusion
   - make notes to speak from
   - each speaker must practise his/her part, especially any difficult language (e.g. pronunciation, expressions)
   - make the visual aids

3. **Rehearse the complete presentation** to make sure you can give it well in the allotted time. Make sure:
   - the introduction and conclusion are interesting and clear

---

Step 4: Before the next session

2.4   Have another rehearsal of your presentation if possible.

SESSION 3

Step 1: Presentation of questionnaire results

3.1   Groups A and B take it in turns to present their findings within 12 minutes.

3.2   The listeners note down any comments/questions to ask at the end.

Step 2: Feedback

3.3   In your two groups, make one list of the strengths of the other group's presentation, and a second list of the weaknesses of your own. Make the lists on OHTs/posters. You might like to consider the following questions:

1) Was the presentation completed within the time limit?
2) Did it hold the audience's interest? Why?/Why not?
3) Was the audience able to follow the presentation? Why?/Why not?

3.4   Present your feedback.

3.5   Note down how the rehearsal helped improve your presentation.

Step 3: Discussion

3.6   Divide into two new groups to consider the following topic: *Should smoking be banned in public places?*
Group 1 will argue in favour of a ban, Group 2 against.

3.7   Prepare your arguments. You might like to consider the following questions:

1) Should the ban be total or partial?
2) Could such a ban be enforced? How?
3) How should offenders be punished?
4) What would the effect of a ban be on the tobacco industry?
5) What is the effect of smoking on health?
6) What is the effect of smoking on the environment?
7) Are there alternative ways of discouraging smoking? What are they?

Try to anticipate your opponents' arguments and counter them.

3.8   Both groups must select two people to put forward the group's arguments in the first part of the discussion, dividing up the points you want to make between the two speakers.

3.9   Choose a chairperson for the discussion. His/her role is to direct the discussion, making sure everyone who wants to contribute gets a chance.

3.10   The two students from both groups put forward their group's view. The listeners note down questions or points they would like to make later.

3.11   The chairperson opens up the discussion to everyone and decides who will speak.

3.12   Vote on the topic.

3.13   Read **Reviewing Discussion: Checklist 3** on page 118 and answer the questions with reference to the discussion you have just had.

Step 4: Language review

3.14 Re-read **Expressing proportion** in the Language Help section on page 136. Add any useful expressions that you have come across in this unit.

3.15 With a partner, think back over the activities you have done in this unit and look at the vocabulary map produced in 1.2. Add any useful words that you have come across related to the topic of Health. Use a dictionary if necessary.

HEALTH QUESTIONNAIRE   A

Part A: Staying healthy

1. How would you describe your diet? Choose one answer.
   a) healthy – lots of nutritious food; little 'harmful' or 'junk' food
   b) mixed – neither particularly healthy nor unhealthy
   c) unhealthy – little nutritious food, a lot of 'harmful' or 'junk' food

2. Is your life
   a) very active (with lots of exercise)?
   b) active (with quite a lot of exercise)?
   c) reasonably active (with some exercise)?
   d) quite inactive (with only a little exercise)?
   e) inactive (with no exercise)?

3. Which of the following are you concerned about with regard to your health? Please tick and add any other concerns at the end, under i) and j).

	very concerned	somewhat concerned	not at all concerned
a) Air pollution			
b) Water pollution			
c) Chemical pollution			
d) Smoking			
e) Passive smoking			
f) Lack of exercise			
g) Diet			
h) Stress			
i)			
j)			

HEALTH QUESTIONNAIRE   **B**

Part B: Attitudes to health care

1. In your country/district, if you are ill where do you go *first* for help?

a) To hospital	d) To a chemist
b) To a doctor	e) To a traditional healer
c) To a nurse	f) Other. Please specify: ....

2. Have you ever had non-western/'alternative' medical treatment (e.g. acupuncture or herbal medicine)?

   YES   NO

   If yes, what kind of treatment was it?

   ....

   ....

   Was it successful?   YES   NO

3. What are the two main health concerns of people in your country/district, e.g. specific illnesses (like malaria) or resources (money, trained personnel)?

   1   ....

   2   ....

LEARNER DIARY SEVEN

Team work

In this unit you received some data (on the completed questionnaire forms). Your group had:

a) to decide on a procedure for processing this data;

b) to process it;

c) to give the presentation.

Thinking of this team-work activity, make notes answering some or all of the following questions:

1. What was easy or difficult at each of the three stages referred to above?

2. If there were problems, what were they caused by (e.g. language, group dynamics)?

3. How would you aim to improve your performance if you did this activity again – or another project involving team work in the future?

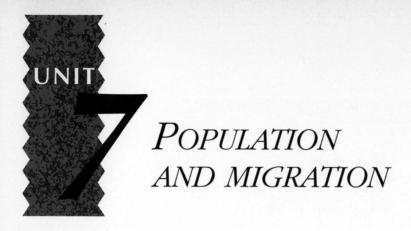

UNIT 7

POPULATION AND MIGRATION

SESSION 1

Step 1: Listening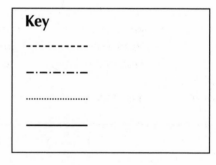

1.1 Listen to a teacher of economics referring to the graph below. Write the names of four countries (France, Germany, Japan and the UK) in the correct order in the key.

UNEMPLOYMENT 1980-92 (AS % OF TOTAL LABOUR FORCE)

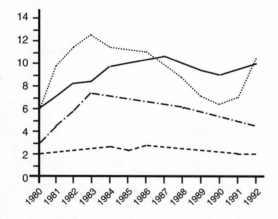

Step 2: Language focus

1.2 Check your answers by consulting the text entitled **Unemployment in OECD Countries 1980–1992** on page 96. Underline the words or expressions in the text that are particularly useful for describing trends.

1.3   Read through **Describing trends** in the Language Help section on page 132 and complete the exercise there.

Step 3: Communication practice

1.4   **Prediction**

Discuss the following questions in your group:

1) Have you any idea of current estimates of world population, or of projections for the twenty-first century?
2) Do you think international migration is on the increase or the decrease?
3) Which country do you think admits more immigrants than any other?

1.5   **Preparation**

Look at the graph indicated by your teacher. It presents information relating to either population or migration. Prepare to give a summary of the information to someone who has not seen the graph. In order to prepare, look back at the strategies listed on page 3 for exchanging information efficiently, and answer the following questions:

1) What exactly is the information presented in this graph?
2) What is the best way to organise the content of your description?
3) What language do you need? Can you find it in **Describing trends** on page 132 of the Language Help section? If you cannot find the language you need there, ask your teacher.

1.6   **Exchanging information**

Pair up with someone who has looked at a different graph. Do not look at your partner's graph. Take it in turns to summarise for each other the information presented in the graphs. As you listen to your partner's summary, note down the main points so that you can refer to them later in this unit. Remember to use **Repair expressions** (see page 139) as appropriate.

Step 4: Discussion

1.7   With your partner, look at each graph in turn and suggest a possible cause of its main feature(s). For example, 'The number of immigrants fell dramatically in 1915. I suppose that was caused, at least in part, by the effects of the First World War[1],0 which must have made international travel more difficult and dangerous at the time.' (See **Cause and effect** in the Language Help section on page 128.)

1.8   Try to think of one or two cases of migration that have received international news coverage in recent months. What were the factors influencing people's decisions to migrate in each case?

[1] 1914–1918

SESSION 2

Step 1: Reading

2.1 Your teacher will give you one of two extracts from a text entitled *Mass migration in the modern era*.[1] As you read it, make notes to complete the worksheet below. You will not be able to complete the whole worksheet at this stage because some of the necessary information is in the other extract. Remember to practise the use of abbreviations and symbols in your notes where appropriate.

2.2 Compare notes with someone who read the same extract as you, and prepare to explain the points you have noted to someone who has not read it.

Step 2: Exchanging information

2.3 Pair up with someone who read a different extract from you. Ask questions to obtain the information necessary to complete the worksheet. When it is your turn to summarise your own extract, refer to your notes if necessary, but do not look back at the text.

WORKSHEET: MASS MIGRATION IN THE MODERN ERA

1. Definition of migration:

2. Factors influencing the decision to migrate:

Factor	Definition/example
push	
pull	
intervening obstacles	
personal	

3. Consequences of migration:

[1] From *The Golden Door: International Migration* by Paul Erlich *et al*, Ballantine 1979.

Step 3: Discussion

2.4 Individually prepare your thoughts for a discussion on the following topic: *Solutions to the world population explosion.*
Write down at least two ideas that you would like to contribute to the discussion.

2.5 Form a group to conduct the discussion. As your group's discussion develops, look for appropriate opportunities to make the points that you wrote down. If possible, relate your point to a point made by a previous speaker.

Step 4: Review

2.6 With a partner, think back over the discussion and your part in it:
- Did you manage to make the points you had intended to?
- If not, what prevented you from doing so?
- What could you or the group have done that would have made the discussion more successful?

SESSION 3

Step 1: Exchanging information

3.1 Form a group with two or three other students. Find out from each other about international migration in the various countries represented in your group.[1] The questions you could ask include the following:
- Is there net immigration or net emigration?
- What are the factors affecting people's decisions to move to or from your country?
- What are the consequences? Are they similar to those described in the text by Erlich *et al*?
- Are there concerns about the consequences of emigration (a braindrain or a labour shortage, for example)?

3.2 In your group, draw up an outline for a five-minute presentation about one of the national (or regional) cases discussed in 3.1.

Step 2: Preparing to respond to questions

3.3 Read through **Responding to questions** in the Language Help section on page 140. Discuss the following questions:
1) In what circumstances following a presentation is the presenter likely to restate or summarise a question before answering it?
2) What is the possible benefit to the audience of his/her doing so?
3) What is the possible benefit to the presenter of his/her doing so?

---

[1] If you and your classmates are all from the *same* country, find out about migration from one region of your country to another.

4) What questions do you think the audience may ask following your group's presentation?

Step 3: Presentation

3.4 Each group in turn gives its presentation. When you listen to another group, note down at least one point you want to ask a question about. When it is your group's turn to respond to a question from the audience, practise restating or summarising the question before answering.

Step 4: Language review

3.5 Re-read **Describing trends** and **Cause and effect** in the Language Help section on pages 132 and 128. Add any useful language you have met in this unit.

3.6 With a partner, think back over the activities you have done in this unit and make a vocabulary map, adding any useful words that you have come across related to the topic of Population and Migration. Use a dictionary if necessary.

LEARNER DIARY EIGHT

Talking about a written text

1. How successfully did you summarise your reading extract for your partner in Session 2?

2. What difficulties did you experience in summarising the reading extract? How far were they affected by: a) your knowledge of the topic; b) the difficulty of the written text; c) the need to convert written text into spoken words; d) other factors?

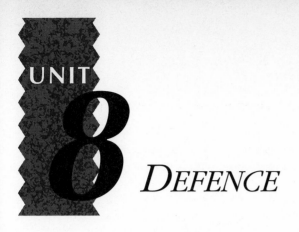

UNIT

8 DEFENCE

SESSION 1

 Step 1: Language practice

1.1 **Preparation:**
1) Form groups of three or four.
2) Look individually at the opinion card that your teacher gives you, without showing it to other members of your group.
3) Prepare to speak for two minutes in support of the opinion written on it. Look through **Expressing opinion** in the Language Help section (page 135) and rehearse some of the phrases you could use.
4) Decide who will go first in your group.
5) Appoint a timekeeper.

NB You do not need to express your real opinions for this exercise; even if you do not agree with the statement on the card, prepare to speak as if it were your own opinion.

1.2 **Giving a talk:**
1) The first speaker then talks for two minutes to express the opinion on the card as forcefully as possible, and to persuade the others to agree with it. When the listeners hear something which they are unclear about or with which they disagree, they can interrupt briefly to ask for clarification (see **Asking for clarification** on page 126) or to express their disagreement (see **Agreeing and disagreeing** on page 125).
2) The timekeeper stops the speaker after two minutes.
3) Repeat the procedure for each speaker in turn.

Step 2: Generating ideas

1.3 In pairs, answer the following questions:
   1) What do you think is the role of a national army in the modern world?
   2) Do you have an army in your country? If so, what is its role? If not, why not?

Step 3: Collecting questions

1.4 Write down two questions of your own about the army in Britain.
   e.g. What is the size of the British army?
      Is there military service in Britain?

1.5 Contribute your questions to the class list of questions.

1.6 Copy down the six questions agreed upon by the whole class to use next session, when you will hear a British army officer talking on this topic.

SESSION 2

Step 1: Listening

2.1 Listen to one of two recordings of Captain Johnson, an officer in the British army. Note down:
   1) any answers to the list of six questions from 1.6.
   2) any other questions asked and the answers to them.

Step 2: Checking

2.2 Discuss your notes from 2.1 with other students who heard the same recording.

Step 3: Second listening

2.3 Listen again and check your notes.

Step 4: Exchanging information

2.4 Work with a partner who heard the other recording. Give your partner the answers to the class questions from your listening text.

2.5 Tell each other about the additional information on your recording and note down any information that is new to you.

Step 5: Before the next session

2.6 If you are from *different* countries, in the next session you are going to tell other students about the national defence forces in your own country.

or

If you are from the *same* country, you are going to have a discussion about national defence in general.

Read the prompt questions under **3. Generate ideas of 'preparing a presentation'** (page 115) and note down your answers or reactions to four of these questions in relation to this topic.

Do not forget to bring these notes to the next session.

SESSION 3

Step 1: Discussion

3.1   If you are from *different* countries, in groups of four or five (as mixed in nationality as possible), tell each other about national defence in your own countries. Use your notes from 2.6.

or

If you are from the *same* country, in groups of four or five, discuss the issues you noted down for 2.6.

You have 30 minutes in total for this group discussion, so make sure each person gets their share of the time available.

Step 2: Review

3.2   At the end of the discussion:

If you are from *different* countries, decide which country's defence you now know most about.

or

If you are from the *same* country, decide which speaker's ideas about national defence you now know most about.

What made that speaker's explanation the most successful?

3.3   Note down two things you will do to improve your own contribution to future discussions.

Step 3: Discussion and reporting back

3.4   As a group, discuss the following:

How will countries defend themselves in the twenty-first century?

Make sure:

- a secretary notes down your group's ideas
- you agree on the grouping and sequence of ideas
- you note down main headings/key points on an OHT or poster

- you have an interesting opening and conclusion
- you have decided who is going to report on the discussion to the class.

3.5   Report back to the rest of the class.

Step 4: Language review

3.6   Re-read **Expressing opinion** on page 135 and **Agreeing and disagreeing** on page 125 of the Language Help section. Add any useful language you have come across in this unit.

3.7   With a partner, think back over the activities you have done in this unit and make a vocabulary map, adding any useful words that you have come across related to the topic of National Defence. Use a dictionary if necessary.

LEARNER DIARY NINE

Talking about a spoken text

1. How successfully did you summarise your part of the spoken text for your partner in 2.4 and 2.5?

2. What difficulties did you experience in summarising the spoken text? How far were they affected by:
   a) your knowledge of the topic;
   b) the way in which the speaker presented the information;
   c) your ability to take good notes while listening for use in speaking;
   d) other factors?

3. Did you find this easier or more difficult than the oral summarising of a written text in Unit 7? Why?

UNIT 9

PARAPSYCHOLOGY

SESSION 1

Step 1: Warm-up

1.1 Discuss the following questions:
1) What is telepathy?
2) Do you believe in it? Why (not)?
3) Do you know of any examples of telepathy?
4) Do you think it is possible to prove whether or not telepathy exists? If so, how?

Step 2: Reading and prediction

1.2 This unit is based on an article published in the *New Scientist* magazine. Read the introductory paragraph, extracted below, and predict with your partner what the rest of the article is about.

Putting telepathy to the test
Psychic research has often been dismissed as the work of cranks[1] and frauds.[2] But now there is one telepathy experiment that leaves even the sceptics scratching their heads.
   Isolated inside a steel-lined cubicle ....

1.3 Read the next two paragraphs of the article on page 54 and answer the following questions with your partner:
1) What is described in paragraph 2?
2) What do most scientists think of research into psychic abilities?

---

[1] A crank is someone who thinks and behaves in an abnormal way.
[2] A fraud is someone who dishonestly presents himself or his work in a misleading way to gain advantage.

Step 3: Before the next session

1.4 The rest of the article has been divided into three texts (A, B and C). Read through the one given to you by your teacher, using a dictionary where necessary. Note your answers to the following questions:

> 1) What are the main points you would need to include to make a clear oral summary of the text for someone who has not read it? (Do not allow your personal opinion of parapsychology to distort the summary.)
>
> 2) Which words would you need to explain or paraphrase?

If there are sections of the text that you find difficult to understand, mark them for discussion in class in the next session.

Do not forget to bring these notes and the text to the next session.

Putting telepathy to the test

Psychic research has often been dismissed as the work of cranks and frauds. But now there is one telepathy experiment that leaves even the sceptics scratching their heads.

Isolated inside a steel-lined cubicle with walls a foot thick, the subject
5 lay back in a chair. Two halves of a ping-pong ball were taped over his eyes and headphones filled his ears with white noise. Three metres away, in a second padded and shielded cubicle, a 'sender' was concentrating on a TV film of an eagle and trying to transmit the image telepathically.

Something seemed to be coming through in the receiver's chamber:
10 "I see a dark shape of a black bird with a very pointed beak, with his wings down ... An almost needle-like beak ... Something that would fly or is flying ... like a parrot with long feathers, on a perch. Lots of feathers, tail feathers ... Flying, a huge eagle. The wings of an eagle spread out." Success: another direct hit for a parapsychology experiment – or so it
15 would appear.

Most scientists view psychic research as the preserve of eccentrics. A hundred years of study, they say, have failed to produce any concrete evidence of psychic abilities. When an experiment has appeared to produce some kind of evidence, it can invariably be explained in terms of
20 a design flaw, a statistical fluke, or cheating. But there is now one experimental result which seems to have at least temporarily impressed the sceptics and which has so caught the imagination of parapsychologists that it will be the subject of no fewer than four replication attempts this year.

From J. McCrone, *Roll up for the telepathy test*, New Scientist, 15th May 1993, page 29.

SESSION 2

Step 1: Language focus

2.1   Look at **Referring to a text** in the Language Help section (page 138). Choose at least two expressions which you think may be useful when you talk about your text in this session and the next. Rehearse these expressions to yourself several times, practising stress and rhythm. Then practise making sentences which refer to your text by using the expressions you have chosen.

Step 2: Discussion

2.2   In a group of people who read the *same* text as you, discuss your answers to the questions in 1.4 and try to reach agreement on them.

2.3   With the help of other members of your group, try to clarify any sections of the text that you marked as difficult in 1.4. If the group remains unclear about any sections, ask your teacher for help.

Step 3: Rehearsal and evaluation

2.4   Pair up with another member of your group to rehearse. Before presenting your summary, tell your partner which aspect(s) of it you would particularly like to have feedback on. For example, you might want feedback on pronunciation (Did the audience find any words difficult to understand because of faulty pronunciation?), or on content (Was it an accurate summary of the original text?), or on the use of an overview and signpost expressions (Did the speaker help the audience to follow the summary?).

   If you prefer, you could ask your partner to give feedback by completing one of the checklists for **Assessing presentations** on pages 112–13.

Step 4: Before the next session

2.5   In the next session you will give the summary to people who have not read your text. Before then, rehearse your summary once again, acting on the feedback that you received in 2.4. If possible, record yourself giving the summary and listen to the recording.

SESSION 3

Step 1: Presenting

3.1   Form a group of three people, consisting of one Text A person, one Text B person, and one Text C person. Give your talks in turn, beginning with Text A. As you

listen, note down for each of the other two talks any points you find particularly:
   1) unclear
   2) interesting
   3) surprising or difficult to believe.

Step 2: At the end of each talk

3.2   Ask any questions about unclear content.

Step 3: At the end of all three talks

3.3   Comment in turn on what you found interesting in the other two talks.

3.4   Comment in turn on anything you found surprising or unbelievable in the other talks. The 'expert' on the relevant text replies to these comments, explaining and trying to justify the claims made in it.

Step 4: Discussion

3.5   What are your own views on this topic now? Note down your answers to the questions below and then prepare to tell other people your views by looking through **Expressing opinion** in the Language Help section on page 135.
   • Do you believe that the existence of psychic abilities, such as telepathy, can be scientifically proved or disproved?
   • Why?
   • Do you have any relevant personal experience?

3.6   Join with other people who are of the *same* opinion as you (either believers or disbelievers in parapsychology). Share your ideas and arguments either in favour of or against the claims of parapsychology. Select one person to present your group's views – including examples from group members' personal experience – to people on the other side of the argument.

3.7   Listen to the two presentations. Consider the persuasiveness of the two speakers' arguments and then vote on whether psychic abilities exist or not.

Step 5: Language review

3.8   Re-read **Referring to a text** and **Expressing opinion** in the Language Help section on pages 138 and 135. Add any useful language you have met in this unit.

3.9   With a partner, think back over the activities you have done in this unit and make a vocabulary map, adding any useful words that you have come across related to the topic of Parapsychology. Use a dictionary if necessary.

LEARNER DIARY TEN

Presenting a point of view

1. In this unit you practised arguing both for your own views (in Session 3) and for a view originally expressed by someone else in a written text (in Session 2). Which of the two do you find easier in English? Why do you think this is?

2. Read the Seminar Instruction Sheet given as an example on page 121. This kind of task (giving a seminar presentation based on your reading of a prescribed text) is common on a wide range of degree courses, particularly at postgraduate level. Have you ever performed this kind of task in your studies, either in your first language or in English? What would you expect to find most difficult about performing the task in English?

UNIT 10

STUDYING IN A
NEW ENVIRONMENT

SESSION 1

Step 1: Warm-up

1.1 Many of you will have been settling into a new environment while using this book - a new college or university, perhaps in a new city or country. Think back over your first few weeks or months in the new environment and note down:
- two things that you have found surprising during your time here
- two things that you have liked
- two things that you have found difficult.

Prepare to explain them to other members of the class.

Step 2: Reading

1.2 A number of psychological studies claim that people's reactions tend to follow a common pattern while they are settling into a new environment. Read the descriptions in the table on page 59 of the five stages identified by Jane Woolfenden.[1] Decide on their chronological order and write the numbers 1 to 5 in the left-hand column of the table.

Step 3: Language focus

1.3 Prepare to explain your answer to 1.2 to your partner. Look at **Deduction** in the Language Help section on page 130 for some expressions that may help you to do so.

1.4 Explain to a partner what you think the chronological sequence of the descriptions is, and why. Discuss any disagreements that arise.

Step 4: Discussion

1.5 In a group, discuss the following questions:
1) Does this model correspond at all to your own most recent experience of

[1] *How to study and live in Britain* published by Northcote House, 1990.

Stage no.	Description of stage
	You thought you had got used to it, but one or two minor things go wrong and it feels as if the whole world is against you. Some people give up at this stage, or become aggressive or withdrawn.
	Excitement.
	Adjustment to the new environment takes place. You either integrate into the new culture, or decide that you don't like it but have to tolerate it temporarily.
	You begin to get used to it.
	Culture shock. A few things start to go wrong. Differences between your own culture and the new culture start to cause problems. What was once new and exciting now seems unfamiliar and frustrating.

      settling down in a new environment?

2) Can you find someone in your group whose personal experience is quite close to the model, and someone else whose experience is quite different from it?

3) Which stage in the process do you think is the most difficult for the person going through the stages? What support or advice would be helpful to the person at that stage?

SESSION 2

Step 1: Listening

2.1 Listen to either Text 1 (Li) or Text 2 (Chris). The speaker in each case is someone who recently completed a postgraduate degree at a British university. They talk about the challenges that face international students, and they offer some advice to those who are about to start a course. Take notes on the advice given by the speaker in your text, so that afterwards you will be able to explain it to someone who has not listened to it.

2.2 Compare notes with someone who listened to the *same* text. Try to clarify between you any uncertainties that arise.

Step 2: Summarising in discussion

2.3 When you are exchanging information or ideas, it can be helpful occasionally to give a very brief summary of what has just been said, before going on to the next point.

Answer the following questions:

1) Do you ever summarise in this way when talking in your first language?
2) At what points in an exchange is it more likely to happen?
3) What purpose(s) does it serve?
4) Which word is most commonly used in English to introduce such a summary?

2.4 Pair up with someone who listened to the *other* text in 2.1. Take it in turns to find out what advice was given in the other text and note the advice down. When your partner is telling you about the other text, wait for an appropriate break between points or sections and then summarise, to check that you have understood the point(s).

2.5 Discuss the relative value of the various pieces of advice, and rank them by numbering them 1, 2, 3, etc. (1 = most important).

Step 3: Group task

2.6 Draft an advice sheet for newly arrived international students who have got only three or four days to settle in before they start a 12-month course at the school or university where you are studying. Make use of the notes you made in the previous exercise and of your own experience.

2.7 Transfer the main headings from your advice sheet to a poster or OHT.

Step 4: Reporting back

2.8 One member of each group presents the group's advice sheet to the whole class, using the poster or OHT prepared in 2.7.

2.9 With the other members of the class, decide which group's advice sheet would actually be of most use to the newly arrived international students.

SESSION 3

Step 1: Assessing your progress

3.1 Estimate your *current* level in each micro-skill listed in the table on the next page. (Circle one number on each line, where 1 = poor and 5 = very good.)

1. Recognising the main point(s) when listening	1	2	3	4	5
2. Indicating when you do not understand	1	2	3	4	5
3. Showing interest	1	2	3	4	5
4. Controlling volume and speed of speaking	1	2	3	4	5
5. Speaking expressively	1	2	3	4	5
6. Selection of content	1	2	3	4	5
7. Organisation of content	1	2	3	4	5
8. Avoiding long hesitations	1	2	3	4	5
9. Avoiding unnecessary repetition	1	2	3	4	5
10. Finding adequate vocabulary	1	2	3	4	5
11. Avoiding grammatical mistakes	1	2	3	4	5
12. Pronunciation of individual sounds	1	2	3	4	5
13. Stress (at word- and sentence-level)	1	2	3	4	5
14. Intonation	1	2	3	4	5
15.	1	2	3	4	5
16.	1	2	3	4	5

3.2 Look at the self-assessment you completed on page 109. Answer the following questions for yourself and then discuss them with a partner:
   1) In which area have you made most progress since the beginning of this course?
   2) In which area have you made least progress? Why?
   3) Are you satisfied with your progress in general?
   4) In which area do you most urgently need to make further progress?

 Step 2: Looking to the future

3.3 Note down your answers to the questions below. You may find it helpful to do this in the form of an ideas-map.
   1) What will you do after this course to continue to improve your speaking skills in English?
   2) What will you do specifically to ensure that you make the further progress that you identified as necessary in 3.2?

3.4 Explain your answers to 3.3 to other members of your group. When the other group members explain their own answers, add to your notes any useful ideas about resources, activities or techniques you could use to continue to improve your English speaking skills after this course.

3.5 Ask your teacher for further ideas to help you continue to improve your speaking skills in English.

REFERENCE SECTION 1

SOURCE MATERIAL

LEGAL IMMIGRANTS ADMITTED TO THE UNITED STATES: FISCAL YEARS 1900–88

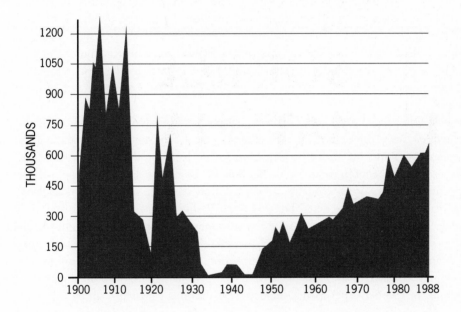

Source: US Immigration and Naturalization Service. *Statistical Yearbook, 1988*. US Government
Printing Office: Washington, D.C., 1989 (xvi).

PUTTING TELEPATHY TO THE TEST – TEXT A

The result came from a series of controversial telepathy experiments carried out over a seven-year period at the Psychophysical Research Laboratories in New Jersey. Chuck Honorton, the researcher behind the experiments, died towards the end of last year of a long-standing heart condition. His mission had always been to put the disreputable field of parapsychology on a

5   firm scientific footing, to design telepathy experiments that could be rigorously interpreted. "I have come to the conclusion that Honorton has done what the sceptics asked, that he has produced results that cannot be due to any obvious experimental flaw," says Susan Blackmore, a psychologist at the University of Western England in Bristol, and a noted debunker of psychic claims. "He has pushed the sceptics like myself into the position of having to say it is either

10   some extraordinary flaw which nobody has thought of, or it is some kind of fraud, or that it is genuine ESP."

Last year, following the closure of his New Jersey laboratory, Honorton joined the parapsychology team at the University of Edinburgh – a research unit founded amidst a blaze of academic disapproval in 1985 with a bequest from Arthur Koestler, the Nobel prize-winning

15   author famous for his belief in paranormal phenomena. Before he died Honorton had been planning a further round of experiments, which will now continue under the guidance of Robert Morris, the head of the unit. The philosophy behind them is straightforward. If psychic powers exist, reasoned Honorton, everyday experience shows that they must be quite weak for most people. So to maximise the chance of seeing these powers under laboratory

20   conditions, investigators should use sensory deprivation techniques. People cut off from everyday sounds and images are more likely to detect psychic signals, or so the argument goes.

In Honorton's earlier experiments, subjects were shut in a ganzfeld, a simple sensory deprivation chamber where bright, red lights are shone onto ping-pong balls taped over the eyes and white noise is played in the ears. For subjects the effect is much like staring into a

25   formless fog. After quarter of an hour or so of such blankness, most people begin to experience brilliant dreamlike images, much like the so-called 'hypnagogic' images that are often seen on the point of falling asleep.

Senders – usually a friend or relative because Honorton believed this would maximise any psychic connection – sat in a second acoustically shielded cubicle. Their task was to

30   transmit the target image: a minute-long sequence of video film that featured either a moving target, such as a clip from an old gangster film, or a static image such as a picture of a landing eagle. The strength of the experiment's design, compared with many previous parapsychology experiments, was that the targets were selected automatically under the control of a computer using a random number generator. This meant that even

35   the experimenter should have no way of knowing which target was being used in a particular trial. A total of 160 targets were used, sorted into groups of four. The computer would pick one group for a session and from this group it would then select a target.

Honorton's belief was that if telepathy existed, the target imagery should turn up in
40 the hypnagogic visions being experienced by subjects in the ganzfeld chamber. Subjects
were asked to describe aloud any images passing through their minds. Both experimenter
and sender were able to listen in on this description over a one-way intercom, allowing
the experimenter to record what was being said and the sender to give extra telepathic
encouragement if the subject appeared to be close to identifying the target image.

DROWSY AND DISORIENTED

45 At the conclusion of a session, the subject would be shown all four images from the group
and asked to pick the one that seemed to best match the imagery experienced in the
ganzfeld chamber. In a step that was later seen as controversial, this judging process was
aided by the researcher, who pointed out correspondences that the subject might
otherwise miss. Honorton felt it essential that the experimenter help the subject, who
50 often emerged somewhat drowsy or disoriented from the experience. To his mind, the
results were not invalidated by this intervention because the experimenter had no idea
which film clips had been used.

If such an experiment were ruled by chance, subjects should pick the correct target
only one in four times – a 'hit rate' of 25 per cent. Honorton was disappointed to find
55 that, despite a few seemingly impressive matches, scoring was not significantly above
chance levels with the static photograph targets (45 hits in 165 trials). But, with the film
and TV clips - a much richer source of target imagery, Honorton argued - the hit rate was
about 40 per cent (77 hits in a total of 190 trials). The chance of this being a statistical
fluke was just two in a million.
60 Some believe the sceptics have failed to give Honorton his due. Blackmore says that if she
had to put her money on the table, she would still guess that psychic abilities do not exist.
However, she feels that while parapsychologists have moved with the times and improved their
methods, the same cannot be said for sceptics. "Their arguments are *ad hominem* and poorly
referenced," she says. "I think a real challenge has now been presented."

Extract from J. McCrone, *Roll up for the telepathy test*, New Scientist, 15th May 1993, pp29-33.

65

WORLD POPULATION GROWTH SINCE 1900

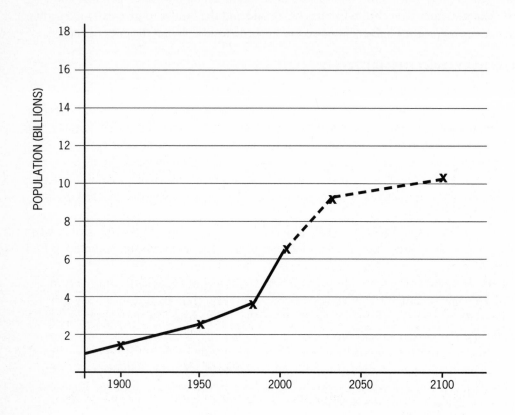

TV PROGRAMMES PRODUCED BY THE BBC 1995

CHART 1: PROGRAMME HOURS BY CATEGORY

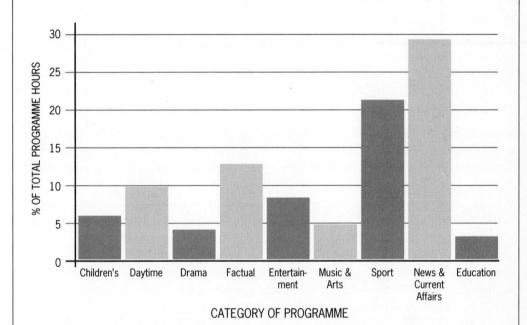

1. Which two categories of programme take up between them over half of the total hours produced?
2. Which is the third largest category as far as hours produced are concerned?
3. Which is the smallest category in terms of programme hours produced?
4. Which three categories of programme account between them for only 12% of the total hours produced?
5. Which feature of Chart 1 do you find most surprising or interesting?

6. Which three categories of programme account between them for only 13% of the total production costs?
7. Which is the largest category in terms of cost?
8. Which are the three next largest categories as far as cost is concerned?
9. Which is the fourth smallest category in terms of cost?
10. Which feature of Chart 2 do you find most surprising or interesting?

THE FAMILY IN BRITAIN
TEXT A

FACES OF THE FAMILY

Our desire to procreate, to parent, to carry on the family name, if a little depleted, remains strong. But which parent? Whose name? Having children has respectably broken beyond the confines of the marital bed. Families have changed their shape, they've thrown up new norms and new dilemmas. Beneath it all, have the foundations really been shaken?

TWO POINT TWO[1]

5   Tabloids[2] suggest that the family structure is disintegrating and the nuclear family has fragmented. In part that's true. The breadwinner dad and stay-at-home mum with two kids reflects the lifestyle of a tiny minority. The most common family form - a married couple with dependent children – accounts for only 40 per cent of the population, although the mum–dad set-up still represents the family experience for the vast majority of
10   British youngsters.

What has really changed is that no one kind of family dominates our society. Families now come in many different guises. There have been two startling trends over the last 20 years or so. The first is the huge increase in the number of children born to parents who are not married. The second is the substantial growth in the number of people living
15   alone. A quarter of all households are made up of single people – twice as many as in 1961. And the fastest-growing group is single men under pension age.

The size of the family unit has also changed significantly. This is partly because of the growth in the number of people living alone and partly because people are having fewer children. In fact, the number of young people has dropped considerably. In 1988 there
20   were 11.5 million under sixteens compared with well over 14 million at the beginning of the 1970s. Fewer couples than ever are producing large families. In the last 30 years, the percentage of households with five or more children has halved to just 8 per cent.

Why is it that despite a one-third drop in infant mortality rates in the last ten years, there are fewer children? One factor has to be that women are producing their babies
25   later. Wider career opportunities, economic independence and later marriage mean that many women, particularly those who are better educated, prefer to let motherhood wait. The longer they leave it, the fewer fertile years they have in which to produce offspring. Some argue that current public and corporate attitudes towards parenting - expensive childcare and few genuine family-friendly policies - along with the inevitable penalties for
30   a break in a career, have made women reluctant to relinquish their hard-won places on the career ladder.

Perhaps also, children hold less significance in women's lives. A survey by the

National Council of Women showed that only 13 per cent of all women of child-bearing age, and one quarter of mothers, agree that a woman needs a child in order to feel fulfilled.

THREE SCORE AND TEN[3]

35   It's not just birth rates that set the pattern of family relationships but also the average life-span. There are currently well over ten and a half million pensioners in Britain. By the second decade of the next century almost a fifth of the population will be aged over 65. That's twice as many older people as in 1950. This tipping of the population scales has far-reaching consequences for the community.

40   At the turn of the century a woman reaching her sixtieth birthday could expect to live for a further 14 or so years; a man, another 13. Today, that same couple could look forward to a further 22 and 18 years respectively. What is critical is the number of men and women living to a very ripe old age. In 1901 there were just 57,000 people aged over 85. A hundred years later that number is expected to top one million.

45   Older people are not a homogeneous group and the picture is very different for men and women. The vast majority of older men are married - even a sizeable proportion of the over-85s. By contrast, only a minority of women are still married over 65. Overall, most older people are living with their spouse. However, the majority of women over 80 live alone. And to prove the extended family is alive and kicking, a sizeable number live

50   with relatives.

        Older people don't just have greater life expectancy than their forebears, they are also fitter and active for more years. A recent survey showed that pensioners have never felt better, many saying they were more satisfied with their life now than in their youth. Clearly older people – a fifth of the population – are not about just to take to the rocking chair.

55   As people continue to live longer, so the number of three- and four-generation families will increase. This will inevitably have an impact on the interaction within the new extended family unit. An ageing population also raises the crucial question about care. If the state can't or won't cope, will the family?

From T. Aleksander, *Faces from the family*, Channel 4 Television, 1994.

[1] Two point two: this refers to the figure (2.2) often quoted for the average number of children per family in Britain.

[2] Tabloids: popular newspapers which tend to sensationalise stories.

[3] Three score and ten: this antiquated form refers to the number of years (70) traditionally considered a full lifespan.

MASS MIGRATION IN
THE MODERN ERA – TEXT A

Migration is usually defined as 'a permanent or semipermanent change of residence'. This broad definition, of course, would include a move across the street or across a city. Our concern is with movement between nations, not with internal migration within nations, although such movements often exceed international movements in volume (especially the contemporary worldwide trend toward urbanisation). Today, the motives of people who move short distances are very similar to those of international migrants.

5

Students of human migration speak of 'push' and 'pull' factors, which influence an individual's decision to move from one place to another. Push factors are associated with the place of origin. A push factor can be as simple and mild a matter as difficulty in finding a suitable job, or as traumatic as religious persecution, war, or severe famine. Obviously, refugees who leave their homes with guns pointed at their heads or with hate-filled mobs at their heels are motivated almost entirely by push factors (although pull factors do influence their choice of destination).

10

Pull factors are those associated with the place of destination. Most often these are economic, such as better job opportunities or the availability of good land to farm. The latter was an important factor in attracting settlers to the United States during the nineteenth century. In general, pull factors add up to an apparently better chance for a good life and material well-being than is offered by the place of origin. When there is a choice between several attractive potential destinations, the deciding factor might be a non-economic consideration such as the presence of relatives, friends, or at least fellow countrymen already established in the new place who are willing to help the newcomer settle in. Considerations of this sort lead to the development of migratory streams.

15

20

From Paul R. Erlich, Loy Bilderback, and Anne H. Erlich, *The Golden Door: International Migration, Mexico and the United States*, New York: Ballantine Books, 1979, pp 10-11.

CHART 1: MALE AND FEMALE STUDENT NUMBERS, BY FACULTY (FIGURES FOR THE UNIVERSITY OF READING, UK, 1995-6)

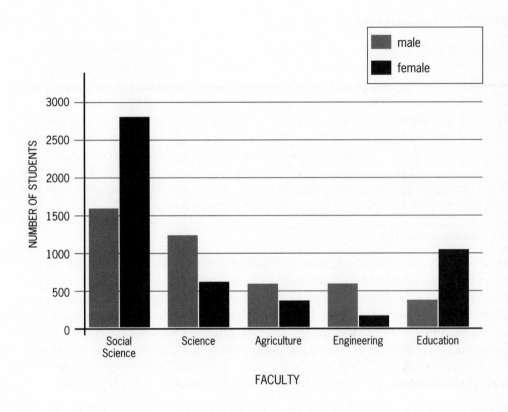

THE FAMILY IN BRITAIN
TEXT B

BRITISH FAMILY LIFE IN THE 1990s

What is clear about Britain in the 1990s is that it is more socially acceptable to have alternative life styles, relationships and ways of bringing up children than it has ever been. It is also easier to remove oneself from an unhappy family situation. In most social groups, divorce is no longer seen as taboo.[1] One-parent families are common. Many children are

5   given more freedom when young; when they move away from home, they move earlier (usually at around 18), and go further. People experiment with relationships before committing themselves to marriage and there is greater acceptance of homosexual relationships. In Britain's multi-cultural society there are many examples of different ways of living. Nowadays, our primary sexual characteristics – whether we are men or women -

10   no longer seem to completely dictate what roles we should take in life.

WORKING MOTHERS

Until relatively recently, most mothers in Britain did not take paid work outside the home. Sometimes women did voluntary work, especially those of the middle classes. However, most women's main (unpaid) labour was to run the home and look after their family. Whether they did this themselves or supervised other people doing it was a matter

15   of class and money. By entering the labour market, women have now altered the face of family life. As the role of the woman in the family changed, so did the role of the man.

EQUALITY IN WORK?

Recent legal changes have given women new opportunities. In 1970, the Equal Pay Act attempted to stop discrimination against women in the field of employment. In 1975 the Sex Discrimination Act was a further attempt to protect women in employment,

20   education and other areas. The 1975 Employment Protection Act gave women the right to maternity leave.

In Britain today women make up 44 per cent of the workforce, and nearly half the mothers with children under five years old are in paid work. It is not uncommon to find that the mother is the main breadwinner.[2] The incentives for women to work or to

25   return to work are increasing all the time, but there are still problems for women who want or have to work.

Although there is a greater acceptance of men taking more of an interest in childcare and domestic duties, studies show that men's and women's roles have not changed as much as could be expected. In most families working women are still mothers, housekeepers

30   and income providers. There is a stigma[3] attached to the phenomenon of 'latch key kids'.[4]

Society expects someone – usually the mother – to be there. Because of the difficulties of combining the mother role with the demands of a career, women's work also tends to be low-paid and irregular.

CHILDCARE

Britain is old-fashioned as regards maternity leave.[5] If they do get maternity leave, women
35 are often worried that, if they do not return to work quickly, they will lose their job and it is often very difficult for them to find another. Paternity leave – time off for the father – is rare, although it is becoming common in other European countries.

A big problem for working mothers in the UK is the low standard of childcare facilities for pre-school children. Parents may employ a nanny[6] to come to their home or
40 to live with them. This is very expensive and only realistic for a small percentage of families. An alternative is childcare centres run by the local council, where a child-minder[7] looks after children during the day in the minder's own home. It is not always easy to get a place in one of these centres.

Once their children have reached school age, most women in Britain work part-time,
45 to fit in with school hours. However, this is not always possible for women who want a career. Recently there has been increasing pressure on the Government to provide more money for state day nurseries, and on employers to establish creches[8] in the workplace.

From C. Addis, *Britain Now, Book One*, BBC English 1992, pp29-31.

[1] taboo: socially unacceptable because it is considered offensive or embarrassing.
[2] breadwinner: person supporting a family financially by earning money.
[3] stigma: a reputation of shame or dishonour.
[4] latch key kids: children who have their own key to their home because there is no one to let them in after school.
[5] maternity leave: paid time off for a woman who is having or caring for a baby.
[6] nanny: child nurse trained to a high standard.
[7] child-minder: a person who is qualified to look after children.
[8] creches: nurseries.

CHART 2: HOME AND INTERNATIONAL STUDENT NUMBERS AT POSTGRADUATE LEVEL, BY FACULTY. (FIGURES FOR ALL FULL-TIME POSTGRADUATE STUDENTS AT THE UNIVERSITY OF READING, UK, 1994–5.)

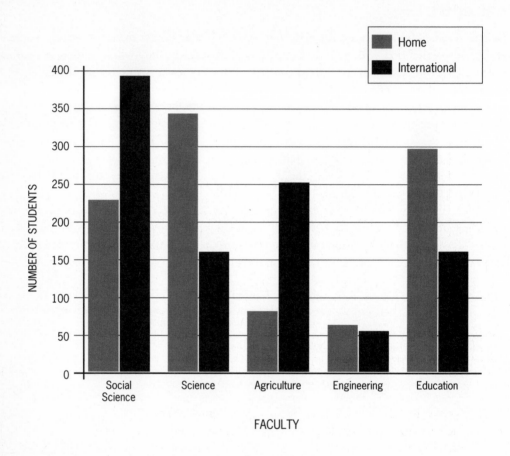

Honorton also went to great lengths to protect against possible collusion between subject and sender. The subject was isolated in an acoustic chamber with walls 30 centimetres thick. The sender's room was less secure but still had four inches of acoustic padding. Copper screening was used as a precaution against concealed radios and the only doors to the cubicles opened onto the experimenter's room.

As well as these physical safeguards, Honorton made methodological changes to protect against deception. Rather than using 'star' subjects – people noted for public performances of psychic abilities – as many previous studies had done, Honorton used over 240 subjects most of whom contributed only a single session. He also used a total of eight experimenters to conduct the sessions.

Honorton published the fruits of his work in 1990 and some more detailed analyses in 1992. Overall, the series produced an average hit rate of 34 per cent compared with the 25 per cent that would be expected by chance.

Back in the University of Edinburgh, Morris agrees that no experiment will ever be fraud-proof. "However, if fraud is the explanation of Honorton's results, it would have to have been a very organised and systematic sort of fraud given the number of subjects and experimenters involved." In any case, he adds, one experiment was never going to decide the existence of paranormal powers. As in any other research field, the evidence will have to be acquired gradually. "We have stopped searching for an instant 'yes' or 'no'," says Morris.

Attention is now turning towards attempts to replicate Honorton's results. As well as the Edinburgh research, ganzfeld systems are being set up in the US and in the Netherlands at university parapsychology institutes. The Edinburgh team plans to start with a copy of Honorton's system, even down to using the same pool of film clips. If they get a positive result, they will vary conditions to try to eliminate some of the more controversial steps, such as the researcher's participation in the judging process. "We would bounce that out and see if the effect persists," says Morris. "Ideally, we would take a transcription of the subject's mentation and submit it for blind judging, letting a third party match the descriptions to the targets."

Eventually, the Edinburgh researchers would also like to perform a series of experiments without a sender: if the telepathy effect is real, they argue, it should disappear in such circumstances. And the influence of personality is another thing Morris and his team are keen to test. Preliminary results suggest that ganzfeld scores might be greater when the sender has an extrovert personality, say the researchers.

Extract from J. McCrone, *Roll up for the telepathy test*, New Scientist, 15th May 1993, pp29-33.

1 Chuck Honorton was the researcher who started the ganzfeld experiments into telepathy, in New Jersey, USA.
2 A ganzfeld is 'a simple sensory deprivation chamber (or small room) where bright, red lights are shone onto ping-pong balls taped over the eyes and white noise is played in the ears'.

MASS MIGRATION IN THE MODERN ERA – TEXT B

Besides push and pull factors, there are what the sociologists call 'intervening obstacles' – deterrents to migration. Even if push and/or pull factors are very strong they still may be outweighed by intervening obstacles, such as the distance of the move, the trouble and cost of moving, the difficulty of entering the new country, and the problems likely to be
5   encountered on arrival.

The decision to move is also influenced by 'personal factors' of the prospective migrant. The same push–pull factors and obstacles operate differently on different people, sometimes because they are at different stages of their lives, or just because of their varying abilities and personalities. The prospect of pulling up stakes[1] and moving to a new and
10 perhaps very strange environment may appear interesting and challenging to a young, footloose man and appallingly difficult to a slightly older man with a wife and young children. Similarly, the need to learn a new language and customs may intrigue one person and frighten another.

Regardless of why people move, migration of large numbers of people causes friction.
15 The United States and other 'receiving' countries (the term used for countries that welcome large numbers of migrants) have experienced adjustment problems with each new wave of immigrants. The newest arrivals are usually given the lowest-paying jobs and are resented by natives who may have to compete with them for those jobs. It has usually taken several decades for each group to gain acceptance in the mainstream of society in the
20 receiving country.

From Paul R. Erlich, Loy Bilderback, and Anne H. Erlich, *The Golden Door: International Migration, Mexico, and the United States,* New York: Ballantine Books, 1979, pp10-11.

---

[1] *to pull up stakes* is an idiomatic expression in American English meaning to pack up one's home.

TV PROGRAMMES PRODUCED BY
THE BBC 1995

CHART 3: PRODUCTION COST PER HOUR

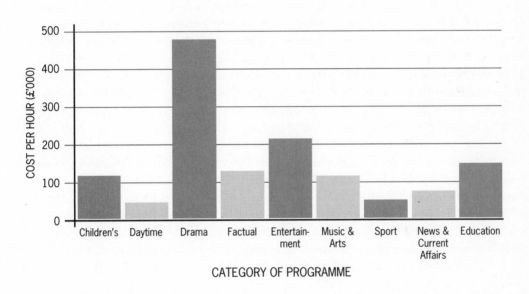

PUTTING TELEPATHY TO THE TEST – TEXT C

Parapsychologists often joke that the last thing they want from an experiment is a positive result. "Immediately you know that either your competency or your honesty is going to be questioned – usually both," said one. Many might argue that this scepticism is well founded. The field of parapsychology has been dogged by a history of wishful thinking and outright cheating. In the 1940s, a British researcher called Samuel Soal claimed great success in the
5   telepathic transmission of numbers. But later, evidence surfaced that Soal had faked his data, altering the target record to match his subjects' guesses. Since then, there have been many other cases of experimenters either fiddling their results or being duped by cheating subjects. A spate of spoon-benders and card manipulators destroyed a number of academic reputations in the 1970s. Sceptics such as the magician James Randi and the former Scientific American
10 columnist Martin Gardner have had a field day rubbishing the work of the gullible researchers. Such is the battering that parapsychology took that, by the end of the 1980s, the field seemed to be in full retreat. Over half the laboratories in the US had to shut their doors as funds dried up, including Honorton's[1] own laboratory. But the study of parapsychology survived and, after its earlier excesses, is now striving to become a model of empirical science.
15   The evolution of Honorton's ganzfeld[2] work is an example of how parapsychology has steadily changed in response to criticism. Ganzfeld experiments began in the mid-1970s and were so popular that, by 1990, nearly 70 studies had been reported. However, the methodology of most of these experiments was so poor that their results were easy to dismiss. In one notorious case, glossy photographic prints were used as targets. Critics pointed out
20 how easy it would have been for subjects to pick out the picture handled during the sending procedure from the fingerprints that would have been all over it. Even without such obvious flaws, most of the studies were based on too small a sample to give statistically significant results.

The reaction of sceptics since the publication of Honorton's results has been mixed. Hyman,[3] the strongest critic of previous ganzfeld work, says he is reserving judgment until
25 there is an independent replication of the results. "Remember, this is only one piece of kit and one lab. The strength of the ganzfeld design was that it was supposed to produce effects that would be straightforward to replicate."

Hyman does concede that the methodological improvements Honorton made present sceptics with their stiffest test to date: "There are a lot of minor things I could quibble with but
30 Honorton met most of the objections I had." Yet the study has not changed his views. He expects time will show that Honorton's results can be explained by some hidden experimental flaw just like so many other parapsychology claims before them. Nicholas Humphrey, a psychologist currently working on a four-year study of parapsychology at the University of Cambridge, is more robust in his criticisms: "The experiments are interesting and somewhat
35 better done than others before them, but they certainly are not foolproof or conclusive ... nobody need take them seriously until there are replications."

FAULTY WIRING

While sceptics have yet to agree on where they think the ganzfeld experiments are flawed, they do see several weaknesses. Humphrey says his most serious concern is over an admission by Honorton that, three-quarters of the way through the experimental series, it was discovered that a faulty soldering connection was allowing the soundtrack of the film sequence being viewed by the sender to leak through the system's wiring into the subject's headphones. Honorton claimed this leakage could have had no effect - even subliminally - as it was only audible with special amplification. Besides, he argued, there was no decrease in scoring once the fault was corrected. But this cuts little ice with Humphrey. "The possibility of leakage means that the early data just have to be discarded," he says, "and when you take those trials out, you don't have enough for a significant result."

Another possible problem with Honorton's findings is that the researchers somehow knew which target segment was playing and deliberately, or even subconsciously, encouraged subjects to select the correct clip during the judging process. The tape counters of the video player used by the system were concealed by nothing more than a cardboard cover and it would have been possible for experimenters to work out which target was playing from a quick peek. Some critics have suggested that even hearing the time it took tapes to rewind may have given away subliminal clues.

Others see the possibility of more direct fraud. Despite the degree of automation, it is conceivable that the record of results could have been tampered with. Each session was taped, the results recorded on the computer's disc. This would make selective recording or fabrication of results difficult rather than impossible. Humphrey stresses, however, that he feels Honorton was an honest investigator and that his results are likely to be the product of an unforeseen flaw rather than deliberate deception.

Extract from J. McCrone, *Roll up for the telepathy test*, New Scientist, 15th May 1993, pp29-33.

1   Chuck Honorton was the researcher who started the ganzfeld experiments into telepathy, in New Jersey, USA.
2   A ganzfeld is 'a simple sensory deprivation chamber (or small room) where bright, red lights are shone onto ping-pong balls taped over the eyes and white noise is played in the ears'.
3   Ray Hyman is a psychologist at the University of Oregon.

REFERENCE SECTION 2

TAPESCRIPTS

FOUNDATION UNIT 3.3

TEXT 1

MR = EAP tutor
JM = Course Leader

MR: Well, thanks for sparing the time to talk to me about your experience of working with international students, John. Would you start by introducing yourself?

JM: My name is John Mitchell. And I am the Course Leader for the MSc in Construction Management.

MR: Now. That's a one-year postgraduate course, isn't it? [Yes] Do you have many international students on the course?

JM: About three-quarters are from overseas this year, which is fairly typical.

MR: Do you find on the whole that your international students have language problems as far as speaking is concerned?

JM: Very few problems, in fact. Only a small minority have problems with spoken English.

MR: What sort of spoken language tasks do they have to do on the course?

JM: Well, there are a number of different kinds of task. If I could start with the first term of the course, one of the first opportunities they will have of speaking English extensively is during an activity called 'Arousal', which is held in the first three weeks. It's a computer simulation, in which the students are invited to run a construction company. They split up into groups of three or four working over a week, trying their best not to bankrupt the company and to keep it in healthy shape. At the end of the week their efforts are evaluated by a team of staff. Because the groups the students work in are mixed in nationality, they will need not only to communicate well but also to relate well to each other. Each group will be expected to give a presentation, and each member of the group will have to tell staff about his/her part in that group activity. So this task during the first week is really quite intensive from the oral point of view.

MR: So that's one type of task. What other kinds of speaking task do they have to do?

JM: Again within the first three weeks of the term, individual students have to decide on the topic they want to write their first essay about and then to discuss this topic with their tutors, explaining why they want to write on that particular topic. One result of this requirement is that we as staff get an indication of each individual's standard of English from the beginning of the term.

MR: I'd like to ask you a bit more about that in a minute. But, just going on through the list of types of speaking task, ...

JM: Right. In the course of terms 1 and 2, students carry out a number of case studies: actual examples from the construction industry.

MR: How long does a case study task take?

JM: It could take a morning, say from 9 o'clock to 12. In the first instance the students would be presented with the case study, and then the latter part of the morning would be occupied with an analysis of the case study, where the lecturer would explore different aspects and ... interrogate, in a sense, members of the class on these particular aspects – ask their opinions, why particular things went well or badly. The lecturer would expect the students to contribute to this evaluation of the case study.

Another task where oral skills are involved is the making of a film, which usually takes place at the beginning of term 2. We're keen that the students should select a particular construction topic and produce a 10-minute film about it. The process of making the film and presenting it to staff involves a considerable amount of working in groups and oral communication. It's not only a question of communicating orally, but of communicating well on a personal level with the other members of your group. We emphasise the importance of group working and we see this in an international context: working with people from different cultures and with different temperaments, but all trying to achieve a common objective within the course.

MR: What about the third term?

JM: I think the major test of a student's communication skills comes in what we call the 'on-site project'. In other words, the department asks one of the major UK construction companies to present the students with a number of problems which the company wants to resolve or would like the students to examine in some detail. So for four weeks students work on-site or at the company's HQ interviewing staff and evaluating the problem. At the end of the month they present their findings to a senior group from the construction company. Now, of course, that is quite a demanding communication task, but we find that the students cope very well indeed. They've had two terms in the department, on campus, living in Reading, and by that time they are usually very fluent indeed.

MR: Is there any advice that you would give to international students starting the course?

JM: As far as oral communication is concerned, I think it really is vitally important that the students should mix widely. I'm certainly keen on the various groups of students mixing and developing their language skills: make use of the opportunity to mix, both in the department and beyond, with students from other countries, with British people, talk to members of staff. Listen to the way language is used in lectures, in the Students' Union. Above all, mix.

(Length of recording: 5 minutes 2 seconds)

FOUNDATION UNIT 3.3

TEXT 2

MR = EAP tutor
CA = Course Supervisor

MR: Well, thanks for sparing the time to talk about your experience of working with international students, Catherine. Would you start by introducing yourself?

CA: Yes, of course. I'm Dr Catherine Andrews. I supervise the MSc in Tropical Agricultural Development, which is a one-year, full-time course.

MR: How many international students do you have?

CA: Well, in the department as a whole: 40, of whom 10 are undergrads. On our MSc programmes about two-thirds of the students are from overseas.

MR: You evidently have a lot of experience of working with international students here. Do you find that they have serious language problems?

CA: On the whole, not. Most of our overseas students come from countries where they have a substantial part of their education in English. For the others there are occasionally some difficulties, but nothing insuperable.

MR: What are the most common language problems?

CA: The most common problem experienced by my overseas students is difficulty in following lectures. I think this is because some of the students, although they may have *read* extensively in their subject in English, have had much more limited practice specifically as *listeners*. As it tends to be the lectures that define the syllabus of the course, it is essential that students should be able to follow the majority of ideas that come across in lectures.

MR: So you would presumably advise them to get as much practice as possible before the course at listening to lectures and taking notes? [Yes, definitely.] What about speaking skills? What kind of speaking activities do they have to carry out during the course?

CA: The way we teach in this department, students are invited to speak a good deal. Even in lectures it's no longer expected that lecturers will do all the talking and students simply listen; lectures are now timetabled in two-hour blocks, which allows the lecturer to invite questions and comments from the students. So, it's very important that, if people don't understand what's being said, they should be able to state what their problem is, or to state clearly their point of view if they disagree with what is being said, all of which is an important part of the educational process.

And the second kind of activity I would mention is presentation. Students will be asked two or three times during their course to lead seminars, by giving a 20-minute presentation to a group of 10 or 15 students and one or two members of staff. They're given several days' or weeks' notice of this and they receive some guidance from their tutor on how to go about it: say, the use of notes rather than a script, for example, or the best use of handouts and visual aids, if appropriate.

MR: Right, you've mentioned two kinds of speaking task so far – responding to lectures and giving seminar presentations. What else do they have to do?

CA: Well, we have a tutorial system, too. Tutorials are occasions where there are normally only two or three students and one member of staff present. The normal format is that the students have been asked to write an essay for the tutorial, and each week one of the students will be asked either to read out his essay or her essay or to speak from the notes that he or she has prepared on the subject. Quite often on these occasions, the students may also be asked to draw a diagram or chart on the board, and simultaneously explain its significance; that requires some precision in getting across ideas, of course, and it's a very valuable skill.

Another task that requires the students to be active and competent speakers is *case study work*, which we use from time to time. We get students into groups and ask them to prepare case studies on certain subjects. Each group will then organise itself, arranging to meet on a number of occasions to thrash out ideas and agree on the main features of the presentation that they would make. And in the end they may be chosen to make a presentation to the rest of the class. So, it's important that everyone feels able to contribute to those discussions, to express their opinions clearly to the rest of the group.

MR: Can you give a simple example of the topic or the nature of one of these case studies?

CA: Well, they may be based on the actual situation in a particular country, or they may be simulations in which each student is assigned a role to play. Our Green Revolution simulation is an example of this, in which some students are farmers, and others are investors, others are agricultural extension officers, and so on. There are many different forms.

The other kind of speaking activity that I would mention is that most overseas students get an oral examination at the end of the course. It's particularly important on these occasions, which can be rather nerve-wracking, that the student should be able to concentrate on demonstrating an understanding of the course content and not be distracted by language difficulties.

MR: Finally, is there any advice you would give to presessional students who were going to come on to your course or similar courses?

CA: Yes, I think the most important thing to understand at the beginning, perhaps, is that the style of the teaching, certainly in my department and I would think in many others, is not a highly formal one. Students are invited to contribute throughout. Most lecturers will be happy to answer questions that arise during the course of lectures or to receive comments or points of view as they go along. You're not going to be in the role of sitting passively through hours and hours of people talking at you: participation by students really is an important part of the process. And clearly, language skills are going to be vital to enable you to make a full contribution.

I also regard the general social activities within the department as an important part of the process of becoming comfortable with the language. We make every effort to meet our students informally, whether it's over coffee, or lunch, or occasionally outside in, say, sporting activities, for example – we've had cricket matches and other sports between Tropical Agriculture and other departments. So, yes, I would certainly encourage students to take advantage of opportunities for informal contact with all their colleagues.

And thirdly, the worst possible thing that someone who has a language problem can do is to conceal it; for example, you know, to sit quietly and miserably in a lecture, understanding very little but reluctant to do anything about it. I know that all members of staff in this department would be sympathetic and would want to support a student in that situation. But, well, we can't help unless we are made aware of the problem, so don't be afraid to approach your tutor about this.

(Length of recording: 7 minutes 58 seconds)

UNIT 2, 1.4

THE HOME IN BRITAIN

Tom: Can I ask you a few questions about the British home? Who lives in a typical home?

Sue: Well, that varies, of course. There's hardly a typical home! Quite a lot of people live alone in Britain – over a quarter of homes are one-person households. The majority of these are retired people who want to keep their independence and live on their own for as long as possible. Another quarter of homes are occupied by married couples with no children. Families with children at home form about a third of all households. The remainder would be single parents with children, unrelated adults (for example, students) sharing accommodation, or extended families.

Tom: How do you pay for your home in Britain?

Sue: Well, although a lot of people rent their homes in Britain, especially single people, most people want to own their homes. And in order to do this, the vast majority of people get a mortgage from a bank or Building Society. This means you have to pay a deposit on the house, but you borrow the rest of the money and then pay it back over a long time; for example, twenty-five years is the usual. Now, the amount you can borrow depends on your annual income. Over 50% of all families live in homes bought with a mortgage, which they hope to pay off by the time the parents reach retirement age. Often monthly mortgage repayments are actually less than the rent for an equivalent property, but, of course, in order to get a mortgage in the first place you have to have a good, regular income and this is a problem for the unemployed or those on low pay.

Tom: Who comes to the home and why?

Sue: Well, this is changing, but traditionally the home is visited every day by the milkman, delivering milk, the newspaper boy or girl and the postman, making their deliveries. Occasionally, door-to-door salesmen may call, selling household goods, things like mops and saucepans, which maybe, you order from a catalogue. Every now and then, people collecting for charity will drop in envelopes for you to put your donations in and then they call to collect them. The window cleaner calls regularly to do the windows.

Who else? Well, there is the unwelcome visitor – a lot of people worry about burglars, and so homes have quite a lot of security devices to keep them out ... Erm, the doctor will come in an emergency, maybe if you can't get to hospital. Elderly people often have home-helps, who come and clean for them and there are district nurses who visit people at home regularly if necessary.

And then there are friends and relatives, of course, who sometimes come for dinner, Sunday lunch, special occasions, maybe like birthdays, New Year, and of course religious festivals – Christmas, the end of Ramadan ... And people with relatives living abroad (Pakistan or Australia, for example), they may have relatives coming from those places and staying for quite a long time. My mother was Australian and we always seemed to have a house full of Australians 'doing Europe' when I was growing up. It was great!

Tom: And what social activities take place in the home in Britain?

Sue: Well, I've already mentioned some – dinners, birthday parties, things like that... Some people with large enough houses and gardens may have their wedding reception in the family home – in a big marquee, a tent, in the back garden. And also, after a funeral; traditionally, people at the funeral are invited back to the house for food and drink.

Some groups of friends will get together in one person's house for a special activity – like playing cards – especially bridge; or watching a special football match maybe or getting a take-away meal and watching a video.

(Length of recording: 4 minutes)

UNIT 3, 1.3

THE ENGLISH EDUCATION SYSTEM

The first point that should be made about the English education system is that it's seen enormous changes since the 1980s. This makes it very difficult to give a clear description of the system that we now have. Today I'm going to do my best to describe the system as I understand it. I'm going to divide my talk into three broad sections: the first part will be
5 looking at the school system itself; the second part will briefly look at tertiary level education in this country – universities; and the third part will consider some of the issues for the future, as I see it.

Right, let's begin with the school system. Schools in England can be broadly divided into two categories. The first is the state school system, which is free to all students, paid for by the
10 state. The second category is the independent or 'public' school system, which is fee-paying. My focus today is going to be on the first category, the state school system, which educates 93% of our pupils, so we're looking here at state schools, not independent or 'public' schools.

So, the state school system. This can broadly be divided into two types of education: there's primary level education and secondary level education. Primary school begins at
15 the age of five in England. Children stay in primary school until the age of 11 and then they change to secondary school, where they must stay until the age of 16. Pupils can choose to leave school at 16 if they want to, or they can stay on at school to complete the final two years of education, which is called the sixth form.

Since 1988 we've had a national curriculum in our state schools, and this specifies the
20 following main points. First of all, there are three core subjects, and these are English, maths and science. All pupils are assessed in these subjects by national tests at certain stages in their education. There are eight other, foundation subjects: history, geography, design and technology and so on, which are not nationally assessed. The national curriculum covers state school studies up to the age of 16, when pupils take what are
25 called the GCSE examinations, that's the General Certificate of Secondary Education.

After the age of 16, pupils who stay on at school and choose to have an academic education, do two years in the sixth form and study for A-levels (that's advanced level examinations). These are taken in just three subjects, three or four subjects only – arts or sciences, usually – and these are the entrance requirements for university.
30 When students reach the age of 16, as I said, they can stay on at school and do A-levels if they want, or they can leave school and attend a college of further education, which will also provide A-level study or more vocational training too.

Students who get satisfactory A-level results can go on to university and that's the second topic I want to look at today. School pupils apply to universities through a central
35 admissions system in their final year of school. Universities either offer them a place which depends upon how they do in their 'A' levels (so they are told, "You must get the following A-level results to get into our university") or they reject them, based upon their school's estimation of their ability and the competition from other pupils. There are 96 universities in the United Kingdom to choose from at the moment and the average full-
40 time undergraduate course lasts three years for most academic subjects, four years for language courses and five for subjects such as medicine and veterinary science.

So let's now turn to the third thing I want to discuss: issues for the future. It's difficult to predict these as there seem to have been so many aspects of education over the last few years that have come to the public's attention. This is because of the dramatic
45 changes in the education system and the many conflicts that arose as a result, in the eighties and early nineties, between teachers and the government. So all this has led to lots of discussion about education standards and priorities, which I am sure will continue. With reference to standards, people will continue to be worried about core skills, particularly in primary school where basic levels of literacy and numeracy must be
50 established. Regarding priorities, another debate that won't go away, I suspect, is about the lack of emphasis our system puts on technical and vocational training as opposed to the more traditional academic education. More important to many parents and teachers will be the priority given to education in terms of funding; people will argue that more

money should go into schools, firstly, to reduce class sizes and, secondly, to ensure that
55 classrooms are well equipped with the latest technology to ensure our school leavers have
the skills needed by an increasingly sophisticated workplace. And last, but by no means
least, attention will be focused on how teachers are selected and trained, as without good
teachers the best system will fail. These seem to me to be some of the main issues for the
future, although I am sure others will also arise.
60 I hope that this quick summary has been useful, but I would like to reiterate my first
point, that really our education system has gone through enormous changes in recent
years. Education has become a very sensitive issue politically and I think it will be very
interesting to see what direction it takes in the future.

(Length of recording: 6 minutes 17 seconds)

UNIT 5, 2.4

TEXT 1

CF = EAP tutor
PC = BBC editor

CF: Could we start with the funding of the BBC? How is it funded and what kind of figures are involved?

PC: The great majority of our funding – in fact, about 95 per cent of it - comes from the licence fee, that is the annual payment which every household that uses a TV set has to make to the BBC. A colour licence currently costs £90, £35 for a black and white set. And last year the BBC collected 21.5 million licence fees, which brought in a net income of £1,660 million. The only other income the BBC has is from its commercial arm called BBC Worldwide, which sells programmes, videos, books, etc., from which the BBC received just £54 million last year.

CF: So the government does not directly control the funding of the BBC?

PC: That's right. The size of the fee is set by the government, usually through negotiation with the BBC; but the government doesn't collect the licence fee money – it's collected by the BBC itself. The only exception to this is the BBC World Service, which is funded by the government's Foreign Office from general taxation.

CF: I'm interested in the question of funding because it must have implications for the independence of the BBC. With these funding arrangements, can the BBC really claim to be independent?

PC: Yes. Yes, I believe it can. Indeed its independence is guaranteed by its Charter. Now, perhaps I could very briefly explain the history or origins of the BBC Charter. The earliest days of television in this country were dominated by an organisation called the British Broadcasting Company, which was created in 1922 and was partly commercial in motivation. People soon began to worry about the new medium's potential for influencing public opinion, and a special parliamentary committee recommended the setting up of a 'highly responsible, independent body to develop broadcasting in the national interest'. As a result, the BBC, that is the British Broadcasting Corporation, was created by Royal Charter in 1927. This Charter, which is reviewed every ten years or so, contains very clear, strict guidelines about the BBC's obligation to remain fair and independent of government.

So, to answer your question, the fact that the public funding of the BBC comes from the licence fee, instead of from general government revenue, allows it to be independent from government pressure, and also, to an extent, from the commercial pressures of the market place. Now, I should perhaps mention that there are very strict rules in the Charter to keep the BBC's main, publicly funded activities separate from the commercial activities of BBC Worldwide which I've mentioned before.

CF: Now, there've been reports recently of major changes in the organisation of the BBC. Has it changed a lot over the last five years or so?

PC: No, no, not as far as its fundamental aims and values are concerned. They remain the same, and it's important that they should continue to do so. But, like every organisation, the BBC studies the conditions in which it has to operate, forecasts how they might change, and then adapts accordingly in order to go on functioning effectively. The BBC is no different in this respect. So, yes, there have been changes, perhaps in two main areas in particular: programme budgets and technology.

Now, the way in which producers spend money on programmes is much more tightly controlled now than it used to be. The basic reason for this is that the income from the licence fee has not kept pace with inflation. At the time of the last Charter review in 1986 the BBC accepted the need for tighter controls on the way it spends its money. It accepted a new obligation in the Charter to have 25 per cent of its programmes made outside the BBC by independent production companies, and the BBC's own producers are required to keep their costs comparable to those of the independents.

Now, some people were worried that this different way of budgeting for programmes might undermine the BBC's traditional public service ethos. On the whole, I don't think that has happened, and I think that a number of good things have come from the change, such as a determination to preserve quality in the areas of programming where the BBC is traditionally strong: Drama is an example of this.

CF: You referred to *two* areas of change.

PC: Yes, the second thing I had in mind was our moving into different kinds of broadcasting, making use of the new technology that's available. Our competitors were ahead of us here in some respects. For many years, until the 1980s, BBC and ITV had enjoyed a comfortable 50-50 domination of the market, but the new broadcasting technology has changed all of that. Satellite TV and Cable TV used by our competitors have eaten into the traditional BBC/ITV division of the market. And unless we take advantage of the opportunities presented by digital technology, we shall lose more of our audience to high quality, interactive programmes on home computers.

So, the BBC has now joined with the manufacturers to develop a digital, satellite TV service, which should be established by the year 2003. It has already launched the country's first digital radio service using satellite technology, which gives crystal clear reception wherever you are in the country, and gives the option for many more stations. Within a year or two we'll all have it in our cars. BBC Worldwide has also developed a lot of multi-media material on CD-Rom, which is expected to become profitable in the next few years. So the new technology certainly does present a challenge for established media organisations like the BBC, but more importantly it offers great opportunities.

(Length of recording: 6 minutes 53 seconds)

UNIT 5, 2.4

TEXT 2

CF =   EAP tutor
PC =   BBC editor

CF: The BBC describes itself as a 'public service broadcaster'. What does that mean in practice?

PC: One aspect of the BBC's public service role is its accessibility. In other words, the BBC makes it easy for the public to contact it and comment on its programmes. Now, there are at least three ways in which the ordinary viewer can do this. Firstly, you can phone or write to the Information Office, which is staffed 16 hours a day, seven days a week, and make your comment.

CF: I see. Is the phone number for that in the phone book?

PC: Yes, it's 0181 743 8000. It's in the phone book, it's in the Radio Times magazine – it's widely available. And people do make use of it and contact us in large numbers. For example, when a controversial programme is shown, thousands phone the BBC TV Centre. Every comment is logged and appears on the desk of the management the next day.

Then secondly, there are our 'rights of reply' programmes, two on TV and one on radio every week, where viewers' comments are discussed. These programmes regularly receive thousands of letters or calls from viewers. And the third route is for people who have especially serious complaints to make; if, for example, someone feels that a programme has invaded his/her privacy or has contained a specific and serious inaccuracy, they should contact the Programme Complaints Unit, which guarantees a reply within ten days of receiving your letter.

CF: Right, erm, how do you make sure that you provide programmes for the whole population, you know, not just one part of it?

PC: Yes, yes, that's another important aspect of our public service function. Well, the BBC is very active in researching its audience: who its viewers are and how they have reacted to particular programmes. There are two main parts to this. Firstly, we organise a Regional Advisory Council in every region of the country. This is a body of a dozen or so people who are selected from the local community. They meet regularly, every six or eight weeks, and their specific role is to advise the TV region or radio station on the output that they've listened to over the previous six or eight weeks: where they think it's going wrong, what changes they'd like to see. Now they don't have any input into the decision-making process on a daily basis, but they are providing valuable feedback, and input into future plans too. We do listen to them and take notice of what they say. After all, we are a publicly funded organisation. People pay their licence fee – they should have a say in what goes out.

Secondly, we commission audience research from independent research agencies, to find out about our audience. They do this using a representative sample of 4,500 homes, where special meters have been attached to the TVs. So, for example – I have some of the figures here – we know that in a typical week last year 94 per cent of the population watched BBC television at one time or another; and that the average viewer watched 25 hours of TV a week, of which 11 hours was BBC. In other words 43 per cent of the average viewer's viewing is of the BBC.

Now, other figures here break the audience down into male and female, into different age groups, and different socio-economic groups.

    Now, because the BBC is a public service organisation, not a commercial one, we aim to serve the wider public by providing a range of programming. For example, in this part of the country there is a large Asian community, and so the local BBC station provides quite a lot of programming with an Asian flavour. And another example, the national structure of BBC Radio also reflects our intention to cater for a broad range of audiences: there's Radio 1 for the youth audience; Radio 2 for an older audience; Radio 3, classical music for a completely different sort of audience not well served by commercial radio; and Radio 4, well ... it's impossible to describe really.

CF: So, as an editor, you presumably have some responsibility for deciding which kinds of material should or should not be broadcast. Do you accept the criticism made by some people, that TV is more violent than it was 20 or 30 years ago, and that as a result our society has become more violent than it used to be?

PC: No. No. I would accept that our society is changing, and that in some respects it may be more violent now. But, is the violence on TV causing these changes, or is it just reflecting changes that have taken place in society? Along with most of my colleagues, I would argue that in our programmes we are merely reflecting what's going on, we're not actually the cause of it.

    The BBC actually has very strict guidelines about what they can show and when they can show it, which all its programme makers have to follow. For example, there's the famous '9 o'clock watershed': programmes that contain more adult material (scenes of sex, violence, bad language) are not allowed to be screened before 9 p.m. The problem there, of course, is: do children go to bed by 9 o'clock these days? And do judgements about adult material change from year to year?

CF: Right, can you give an example of an editorial decision not to screen something, and explain the reasoning behind it?

PC: Yes, of course. In News and Current Affairs, picture editors are taking decisions every day about what they should and shouldn't show. The BBC receives large numbers of pictures every day from news agencies around the world and also from its reporters in war zones, for example Bosnia in the early 1990s, which would be considered too strong to show on domestic TV news. Now some of these pictures would be shown in certain other countries, say France, Germany or Italy, where there are different standards about showing bodies and bits of bodies.

CF: Why should that be? Does the BBC think the British are more sensitive, that we need more protection?

PC: No, I think it's a question of what is to be gained by showing such scenes. I mean, as long as you've got a reporter who can convey effectively in *words* the horror of the incident, it isn't necessary to show pictures of the most gruesome details. And there is also the worry about desensitisation: if horrific scenes are shown in close-up night after night, people might become immune to the horror after a while, and then the impact of it would be lost.

(Length of recording: 7 minutes 42 seconds)

UNIT 7, 1.1

UNEMPLOYMENT IN OECD COUNTRIES 1980-1992

... so the debate about whether governments can create real jobs will continue. Let's look now at the experience of different countries.

This graph shows the changing levels of unemployment over the period 1980 to 1992 in four OECD countries: France, Germany, Japan and the UK. Of the four, Japan had the lowest level; unemployment remained fairly stable there, at between 2 per cent and 3 per cent throughout this period.

As you can see, this contrasted quite sharply with the UK. Unemployment here was relatively high and fluctuated considerably. It rose steeply from 6 per cent in 1980 to a peak of just over 12 per cent in 1983. It fell back in the late '80s, but then increased sharply again in the last two or three years of the period.

As in the UK case, Germany's unemployment peaked in 1983, though at the lower level of 7.5 per cent. However, the subsequent fall, to 6 per cent in 1988 and 4.5 per cent in 1992, was steadier and longer-lived.

In France, unemployment peaked comparatively late, in 1986-7. After a slight fall it was once again on an upward trend after 1990.

What steps did the governments of these countries take to deal with unemployment? Well, if we look first at the UK, ...

(Length of recording: 1 minute 45 seconds)

UNIT 8, 2.1

EXTRACT A

Mike: Captain Johnson, I'd like to ask you some questions about the British army. Can I start by asking you about the role of the army in Britain today?

Capt J: The role of the army in Britain today is primarily as a defence force. A lot of the time is spent in mainland Britain training – always in preparation for any conflict we may be called to assist in. In Northern Ireland, however, we have a completely different role and we are there as a result of the Troubles in 1969, which some people may have read about, and we are there to assist the Royal Ulster Constabulary in the maintenance of law and order – so it's not entirely a defence role and certainly not a war situation in our perception – we're there assisting the police force in Northern Ireland.

Mike: And can you tell me, what's the role of the British army, firstly, within NATO and, secondly, within the United Nations, the UN?

Capt J: Our membership of the North Atlantic Treaty Organisation dates back to the Second World War and we're there as part of an agreement with the other countries (for example, France, Canada, the United States) and the agreement was that, should any member state be invaded or be under threat of invasion, the other countries would assist. Well, thankfully, now that threat is decreasing in our perception in the Western World and so NATO is very much more a political organisation and it aims to improve the standards within its member countries in all aspects of life, not necessarily just in defence.

Our role within the United Nations again is very similar but in more recent times we've taken on very much peacekeeping duties; for example, we have an ongoing role in Cyprus where we provide troops for what is known as the Green Line that divides the Greek Cypriots and the Turkish Cypriots and that's been going on since 1974.

In the early nineties we had a role in the former Yugoslavia assisting the United Nations again in a peacekeeping role to try to maintain the aid corridors so that we could help the people who were affected by the civil war there.

Mike: Thank you, and, finally, what challenges do you think there will be for the British army in the next hundred years? How will it change, do you think?

Capt J: Well, personally, I find that very difficult to predict because so much has happened over the past fifty years in Western Europe and even more recently – I mean, for example, no one would hardly have dared imagine in the early eighties the changes that would arise in the former Soviet Union. I think the challenge for the British army every year is keeping pace with the changes in the world. I couldn't even say where a threat might be or where we might be called to assist. I think the challenge is simply keeping up with world events and maintaining our defence role.

Mike: Thank you very much, Captain.

(Length of recording: 2 minutes 59 seconds)

UNIT 8, 2.1

EXTRACT B

Mike: Can you tell me who joins the army?

Capt J: Who joins?

Mike: In Britain?

Capt J: Well, we, er, the army takes applicants between the ages of sixteen and a half and 24, although that age – the maximum age – can increase to 32 depending on the qualifications that the individual has. We take people with the minimum qualification of five GCSEs for officer entry and in all our soldier trades it is three to five GCSEs depending on the kind of job they want to do. We've got no discrimination against any sector of society; if they have the correct qualification educationally and they satisfy our medical criteria, because, obviously, we need fit people, and they pass all the selection, we will take the most suitable applicant.

Mike: Uhm, we don't have military service in Britain. What do you think are the advantages of having a professional army over – er – a conscripted army?

Capt J: Well, you are quite right, we *are* a volunteer force – there are no forced men or women, so we think the advantage is that we get people into the army who *do* want to join. I have no experience of conscripted armies and I have never served alongside any so it'd be unfair of me really to say that we are better or worse. But my understanding, from the time that I spent abroad, is that the British army *is* held in very high regard because we are a volunteer force. I think that we have better continuity because we do have people in the army for longer periods of time. While the minimum service is three years, an average soldier will serve six to nine years and an officer will serve approximately six to eight years. So we do have that continuity which a conscript army may not necessarily have, in such great numbers. Obviously, they will have their training staff, but the majority of their workforce will be leaving after very short periods of time.

Mike: Right. Can you tell me who controls the army?

Capt J: Who controls the army?! Well, the King or Queen of the day is officially Commander in Chief of the army. But, of course, in practice, because we are a parliamentary democracy, it is the government of the day that controls the armed forces. This is done through the Ministry of Defence.

Mike: And how is the army paid for?

Capt J: Again, by the government. The funding for the Ministry of Defence comes out of the public sector budget, so we take our share alongside Health, Social Security and Education. Our share will probably not increase by a great deal over the coming years because of the changing role of the army, because of the reflection of a more stable Western Europe.

Mike: And how many people are in the British army at the moment – approximately?

Capt J: Well, approximately 150,000 are serving in the British army today.

Mike: Thank you very much, Captain Johnson. That was most interesting.

Capt J: You're most welcome.

(Length of recording: 3 minutes 2 seconds)

UNIT 10, 2.1

TEXT 1

MR = EAP tutor
LY = international student

MR: Hello, Li. Thanks for agreeing to come and talk about the experience of studying here as an international student. You're just finishing a one-year Masters course, aren't you? [Yes, that's right.] What has it been like for you, working with British and other international students together?

LY: Well, it has been a new kind of experience for me. Everything was new to me at the beginning. But as in any new situation, I gradually learned to adapt. I think that, if you're studying at a university with people from all over the world, you need to accept that there will be cultural differences between people, and you need to be tolerant of them so that you can get along with people well enough to work with them. Oh, and, of course, it's right to expect other people to show a similar acceptance and tolerance towards you.

MR: Yes, I know that students are sometimes advised to form study groups with others on the course. Did you do that, and, if so, was it helpful?

LY: Yes, I agree that it's a good idea. But of course it doesn't work with just anybody. I think it's worth looking for people who have similar study habits to your own, and if possible people who don't live too far away from you. And again you have to be prepared to be flexible; to adjust your own approach a little sometimes, so that it's easier for the other people to work with you.

MR: Now, what about the tutor? When you started your course, was it clear to you how to approach the tutor and what for?

LY: I think the responsibilities of the tutor are written in the department's handbook [That's good.] So the student should read that to get a basic idea of the support she is entitled to expect from her tutor. But you need to play it by ear a little at first, because obviously tutors are human and so they are different. You have to approach different tutors in different ways. One point I would make about meetings with your tutor is: it is worth preparing a little bit before the meeting – working out the questions you want to ask and the kind of answers you expect or need, so that you make the best possible use of the time during the meeting. Personally, I take in a list of points in order of priority: like 1, 2, 3, 4, etc.

MR: Apart from your tutor and fellow students, what other resources have you made use of during your period of study?

LY: Well, I would advise any new student to explore the university campus thoroughly early on in her stay, if possible with some guidance from a more experienced student to get to know the facilities that are available. The first place I explored was the library – it's important to find which parts of the library are particularly relevant to your subject area, and to discover whether there are other, specialist libraries or collections in some departments. For example, in my case, there were books on linguistics in one part of the main library, periodicals in the other part, and then there was the departmental library and also a useful library in a neighbouring college. It took a while to discover where everything was.

   But the library is not the only facility which is open to all students, of all departments: some departments or units run an advisory service. This means that at certain times of the day students from any department can go along and ask for help with their project. It's well worthwhile asking about these advisory services early on in your course, and don't be afraid to make use of them – they are there to help students, that's their function.

MR: Did you use these advisory services yourself?

LY: Oh, yes, two of them. The advisory service in the Computer Centre has helped me several times: once when my disk was stuck, and another time when I thought I'd lost a lot of data ... And the Applied Statistics department also runs an advisory service, which I would recommend to anyone who is going to do experimental research. The staff there will discuss the design of your experiment with you – of course, you should do this early on in your project at the planning stage, so that it's not too late to make any changes that they suggest. They will also help you analyse the data later on.

MR: Right. The facilities you've mentioned so far have been broadly academic. What other kinds would you advise new students to make use of?

LY: They should make use of the Students' Union of course; after all, it is supposed to be run by the students for the students. It has an Overseas Students Committee, which is made up of people who have already been in the UK for a year or two and want to use their experience to improve the services provided for overseas students. You can contact them at the Students' Union.

   Another good reason for visiting the Union, as well as the shops, is that it is the information centre for the various university clubs or groups, and for student activities in general. In one part of the building there are several big notice boards, where groups can advertise forthcoming events and sometimes a list for people to sign up if they are interested in a particular activity. There are also boards for other kinds of notice: for example, people who want to share accommodation, or second-hand books for sale.

MR: I imagine those groups are a good way for overseas students to meet British students, for social reasons and also perhaps to practise speaking English. [Yes, I agree.] Did you do that yourself? Did you join one of these clubs?

LY: Oh yes, I joined the Chess Club. That was a good move, because sometimes you need a place where you can get right away from your academic studies for a while. Chess is always refreshing; you sit down and ... I guess you use a different part of the brain. And as well as the chess itself, there is the social contact. People tend to talk a lot at our chess evenings; maybe not so much during, but before and after their games; not just about chess – all kinds of things.

MR: And what about sports? I know there are quite a lot of sports clubs advertised on the notice boards as well.

LY: Yes, there are various sports, and the one I'm interested in is mountaineering. [Mountaineering!] Yes. It can be quite demanding. But it gives you a sense of satisfaction when you climb ... the highest mountain in Wales, for example.

MR: I'll have to take your word for that. Right, finally, is there any advice that you wish you'd had at the beginning of your course?

LY: Yes, to be prepared for a style of lecture in which contributions from the audience are often invited by the lecturer. If you are not used to this style, it can at first seem off-putting, even aggressive. Try to practise contributing so that you can join in the discussion.

Perhaps I should explain that, although contributions to the class discussion were encouraged, it was certainly not acceptable for a student to engage in private discussion with the one or two people nearest to him during a lecture. That happened a couple of times in the first week of my course, and it was an irritating distraction for the lecturer and all the other students.

One final point: make an effort to see the course as a whole from the start. If, as in my case, the most important part of the course in terms of both assessment and learning is a dissertation project, use the early parts of the course to prepare for the dissertation. Jot down ideas about it from time to time, to help you gradually work towards it.

MR: Right, well, thank you very much, Li. You've been very helpful.

LY: It was a pleasure.

(Length of recording: 8 minutes 37 seconds)

UNIT 10, 2.1

TEXT 2

AT = EAP tutor
CG = British student

AT: Now, Chris, can I get this right: you've just completed an MSc course on which a large proportion of the students were international students? Is that right?

CG: That's it. Yes, I was in AERD – that's the department of Agricultural Extension and Rural Development.

AT: And how do you think the students from other countries got on on that course?

CG: Pretty well. I think we found as the course went on that we were all in the same boat really. For example, the majority of both home and international students were returning to full-time study after several years in work. That was an important thing to have in common.

AT: What advice would you give students, particularly international students, based on your experience as a student here?

CG: I think the most basic thing is to make use, full use, of your tutors and lecturers. Maybe some of the overseas students, perhaps even some of the home students, don't do that. They're a bit too shy early on of taking questions or problems to tutors or of making use of the time that tutors make available. So, the first piece of advice I'd give, I think, is to find out at the beginning of your course the times at which your tutor is going to be available for tutorial appointments, and then make full use of them.

AT: So: any problems, they should tell the tutor as soon as possible? [Yes.] And, of course, if they're in a department where they don't have a personal tutor, I suppose they should go to the lecturer concerned. Moving on, what about the amount of reading that you have to do as a university student?

CG: Yes! It looked pretty daunting at first, with those long reading lists. I think the important point here is to be selective: don't think that you have to read everything that's listed – you're not expected to. Find out which are the most important items on the list – ask the lecturer or tutor if necessary, and then, if your time is limited, spend it reading those books thoroughly.

AT: What about study resources on the campus – the library, for example, any tips there?

CG: Yes, make use of the recall system. If, when you get to the library, you find that the particular books you need have been borrowed by someone else, don't give up. Fill out a recall slip, hand it in at the information desk, and within a few days the library will contact you to tell you the book is now ready to collect. Once I discovered this system, unfortunately not until half-way through my course, I used it a lot and I found it very helpful. Of course, it means you need to plan your work properly; it's no good leaving the essential reading for an assignment until just before the deadline, and then, then trying to use the recall system – it's too late then.

AT: Any advice on working with other students?

CG: When you are given an assignment, definitely talk to your fellow students about it: discuss your initial ideas about it, and then later how you're getting on with it, what you're finding difficult, etc. This will help you to think around the topic, and will also reassure you that you are not the only person feeling the strain.

And if you feel keen, you can try setting up a study group with some of the others. On our course, for example, five of us formed a study group in the second term and worked together on revising for the exams. But a study group can be helpful at any point in the course – for a particular assignment, for instance. You need to work out which of the other students on your course you find it easy to work with, maybe people who have the same approach to study as you, or simply people who live in the same hall of residence as you. I got together with four others and we decided that we could do the reading for the exams more enjoyably and more efficiently by sharing it. So we agreed which person should read which item on the list, and then we met up once or twice a week after lectures and summarised our reading for each other. And when someone wasn't clear about something, or disagreed with something, we discussed it. I learned a lot from that. It also made me more confident about expressing my ideas, as you need to do in seminars.

AT: So, try to form a study group with other students to share the workload. [Yes.] Now, what about choosing options? That's often a very important part of a course, making selections about exactly what you will study. Any advice there?

CG: One point I would make is, perhaps it's obvious: choose options according to which subject interests you, not according to who the lecturer is. Don't choose an option simply because it's organised by someone who gives nice, clear lectures. There may be a greater risk of some overseas students making this mistake because they are so concerned about understanding every word of a lecture. But we all agreed, at the end of our course, that the subject, not the lecturer, should be the most important consideration when you choose options. If you choose a subject that really interests you, it is quite likely to provide you with a dissertation topic that you are really motivated to work on. [Right, well that's ...] So, go for the subject not the lecturer.

AT: That's my next question, actually! Any advice on writing the dissertation – if you're a postgraduate – or an extended essay if you're an undergraduate?

CG: As soon as you have drafted a proposal, an outline of what you intend to write about, have a meeting with your tutor or supervisor to establish whether the basic idea is viable. This is important because otherwise you might spend days working on a project, only to discover at a later stage that a supervisor has some basic objection to what you're doing, and that you have wasted a lot of time. So, have an early meeting to get some official feedback on your proposal.

One other point about working on a major project, such as a dissertation: draw up a work schedule at the beginning, with reasonable deadlines by which you intend to complete each stage of the project. The project can seem like a huge mountain to climb at first, so it's good for morale if you divide it up into manageable sections: 'I'll finish reading by the end of April, I'll complete data collection by mid–May, and then I'll write the first two chapters by the end of May'; that kind of thing. Even if you don't meet all the deadlines, you will have a sense of progress.

AT: OK, that's very helpful, Chris. Thank you very much.

CG: No, not at all.

(Length of recording: 7 minutes 2 seconds)

INDEPENDENT LEARNER

LEARNER QUESTIONNAIRE

PART ONE

1. Feelings
How do you feel about communicating orally in English? (Circle one of the given options, or add a more appropriate one.)

I feel   a sense of achievement

excited

nervous

impatient

frustrated

....

2. Previous experience
2.1 Over the last 12 months, how much practice have you had at communicating orally in English outside the language classroom? (Tick one column in each line.)

	NEVER	OCCASIONALLY	FREQUENTLY
1. Conversation (with one other person)			
2. Conversation (in a group)			
3. Informal discussion with colleague(s)			
4. Making a presentation to colleagues			
5. Questioning a speaker on his/her presentation			
6. More formal academic discussion			

2.2 Which of the above do you find relatively easy or difficult? Why?

EASY	DIFFICULT

3. Picturing the target skills

3.1 Do you think it will be important during your academic course to be able to communicate well orally? For what sort of purpose or task?

3.2 Will oral communication in English be important outside the academic context? For what sort of purpose?

4. Analysing the target skills

How important do you think the following are in achieving effective oral communication? (Tick one of the three columns in each line.)

	NOT VERY	QUITE	VERY
Recognising the main point(s) when listening			
Indicating when you do not understand			
Showing interest			
Controlling volume and speed of speaking			
Speaking expressively			
Selection of content			
Organisation of content			
Avoiding long hesitations			
Avoiding unnecessary repetition			
Finding adequate vocabulary			
Avoiding grammatical mistakes			
Pronunciation of individual sounds			
Stress (at word- and sentence-level)			
Intonation			
....			
....			

5.   Initial self-assessment

What are your own strengths and weaknesses in oral communication in English at present? Estimate your own level in each of the micro-skills listed below. (Circle one number in each line, where 1 = poor and 5 = very good.)

1. Recognising the main point(s) when listening	1	2	3	4	5
2. Indicating when you do not understand	1	2	3	4	5
3. Showing interest	1	2	3	4	5
4. Controlling volume and speed of speaking	1	2	3	4	5
5. Speaking expressively	1	2	3	4	5
6. Selection of content	1	2	3	4	5
7. Organisation of content	1	2	3	4	5
8. Avoiding long hesitations	1	2	3	4	5
9. Avoiding unnecessary repetition	1	2	3	4	5
10. Finding adequate vocabulary	1	2	3	4	5
11. Avoiding grammatical mistakes	1	2	3	4	5
12. Pronunciation of individual sounds	1	2	3	4	5
13. Stress (at word- and sentence-level)	1	2	3	4	5
14. Intonation	1	2	3	4	5
15.	1	2	3	4	5
16.	1	2	3	4	5

PART TWO

6.   Setting objectives

6.1   What do you intend to be able to do well by the end of the course which you have difficulty with at present?

6.2   What in particular are you going to concentrate on improving in the first half of the course?

6.3   What will be your 'measure of success'? (In other words, how will you know whether you have achieved the improvement referred to in 6.2?)

7.   Action

What practical steps are you going to take in the next week in order to make the improvement referred to in 6.2?

KEEPING A
LEARNER DIARY

Research suggests that foreign language learners benefit from reflecting on their learning. The process of reflection involves trying to answer questions such as: What do you need to learn? What are your strengths and weaknesses? Which way of learning suits you best? How well are you progressing? What techniques can you use to make further progress?

One way of exploring these questions is to keep a Learner Diary. There is a task at the end of each unit, where you are asked to note down your thoughts in relation to a particular aspect of the work you are doing on the course (for example, **Expanding your vocabulary** or **Taking part in a discussion**). Each Learner Diary section contains questions intended to stimulate and help you direct your thoughts on the theme. You do not need to answer all of the questions; concentrate on those that interest you most, and generate others of your own.

Writing about your learning like this may be new to you, and may therefore seem strange at first, but we strongly advise you to try it. Students have been interested, and sometimes surprised, when they re-read their diaries at the end of the course, to notice how their understanding of their own learning has developed.

Find 10 or 15 minutes at the end of each unit to think and write about the diary theme. Keep a notebook or file especially for this purpose. As it is a diary, you do not need to write in perfect sentences; the priority is to get your ideas down on paper, so write in whatever style enables you to do that most easily.

You can keep your diary private, for your attention only. Alternatively, you can discuss parts of it with a fellow student or with your teacher. Showing the diary to your teacher can help him/her to understand what kind of guidance or practice you would benefit from.

On the next page are two examples of diary entries:

LEARNER DIARY FOUR

1997 NOVEMBER

---

5 WEDNESDAY

Pronunciation

I have improved my fluency over the past few weeks, but I am still worried about my pronunciation. I shall record myself speaking next week and try to identify specific pronunciation problems to work on.

LEARNER DIARY FIVE

1997 NOVEMBER

---

7 FRIDAY

Taking part in a discussion

I have always found it difficult to take part in discussions in English. This week I have tried to improve my discussion skills by preparing more carefully: before the discussion starts I write down two or three points I want to make during the discussion. This strategy seems to have worked quite well for me this week: I have found it easier to take part, because I have something definite to say and I feel more confident than I used to.

Sometimes, however, the discussion did not get round to the subject I wanted to discuss, and I wasn't sure how to change the subject. How do other people do it? I'll try to listen to them and find out.

ASSESSING PRESENTATIONS: CHECKLIST 1

1. Was the presentation interesting?	no / quite / yes
2. Did the speaker help you to follow the main points?	no / a little / yes
3. If posters or OHTs were used, were they clear?	no / quite / yes
4. Did the speaker maintain sufficient eye-contact with the audience?	no / yes
5. Comment on the speaker's voice: a) speed b) volume c) pitch variation	 too fast / too slow / about right too quiet / about right monotonous / expressive
6. Did the speaker help the audience to understand any unusual words that were used?	no / yes
7. What could the speaker do to improve the presentation next time?	

ASSESSING PRESENTATIONS: CHECKLIST 2

1. Was the presentation interesting?	no / quite / yes
2. Did the speaker help you to follow the main points?	no / yes
3. If OHTs/posters were used, were they: a) legible?	no / quite / yes
b) understandable?	no / quite / yes
4. Did the speaker maintain sufficient eye-contact with the audience?	no / yes
5. Comment on the speaker's voice: a) speed	too fast / too slow / about right
b) volume	too quiet / about right
c) pitch variation	monotonous / expressive
6. Did the speaker help the audience to understand any unusual words that were used?	no / yes
7. Did the speaker manage the timing well?	no / quite / yes
8. Did the speaker deal with questions well?	no / quite / yes
9. Did the speaker conclude satisfactorily?	no / yes
10. What could the speaker do to improve the presentation next time?	

PREPARING A PRESENTATION: IMPROVING SKILLS

(See prompt-questions on pages 115-117 for further details.)

PHASE 1: DEFINE THE TASK
STEP 1   Define presentation task
STEP 2   Identify learning purpose

PHASE 2: EXPLORE THE TOPIC
STEP 3   Generate ideas
STEP 4   Look for shaping idea
STEP 5   Collect information
→ Have you found: 1) material to interest the audience? 2) your main point or idea to shape the material? NO: return to Step 3.   YES: go on to Step 6.

PHASE 3: PREPARE FOR THE AUDIENCE
STEP 6   Draft outline
STEP 7   Draft aids
STEP 8   Rehearse and evaluate
STEP 9   Revise outline and aids
STEP 10 Present

PHASE 4: REVIEW
STEP 11 Seek feedback on performance
STEP 12 Review learning

PREPARING A PRESENTATION: PROMPT QUESTIONS

1. Define presentation task

What is the purpose of the presentation?
Who is your audience to be?
How long is the presentation to last?
Where is it to take place and what aids will be available?
How long have you got to prepare the presentation?
What is the topic to be?

2. Identify learning purpose

Which aspect of presentation do you particularly want to improve?
What will your criteria of success be?

3. Generate ideas

What is interesting about the topic?
What would you/the audience like to find out about the topic?
What questions do people ask about the topic?
What is the mainstream view of the topic? What is questionable about this
    mainstream view?
What alternative views are there? What is questionable about these alternative views?
What is controversial about the topic?
What is new or the focus of current debate?
What misconceptions are there about the topic?
What about the topic is surprising to you, or would be to the audience?
What unexpected links are there within or beyond the topic?

4. Look for shaping idea

What is the question you want your presentation as a whole to answer?
What is the main, overall point you want to make?
What view of the topic are you proposing?
What is your line of argument?
What conclusion are you leading towards?

5. Collect information

What important gaps are there in your knowledge?
At which points does your information/argument seem to be lacking?
What information do you need in order to illustrate/support/develop a point?
Who or what could be the most valuable source of information and ideas on the
   topic?

6. Draft outline

How many major points can an audience take in during an X-minute presentation?
What are the three or four most important points for you to get across to your
   audience?
What is the best order to present the points in?
What would be an effective opening?
How will you conclude?
Is the overall structure clear and logical?

7. Draft aids

What headings will you use in your overview to guide the audience (and yourself)?
What essential information do you need for your own use on prompt cards/
   prompt sheet?
Which information is best conveyed visually (e.g. overview, statistics, process)?
What is the best way of conveying it visually (e.g. diagram, picture, map, text; on
   board, OHT or handout)?
Which information (if any) is best given on a handout? At what point is the
   handout to be distributed? What do you want the audience to do with it?

8. Rehearse and evaluate

Did you manage to complete the presentation within the time-limit? If not, what
   will you cut out?
Did you hold the audience's interest? If not, why not?
Was the audience able to follow the presentation? If not, why not?
Was the audience able to note down your main points? If not, why not?
If the audience asked questions, did you answer them effectively? If not, how
   could you do so next time?

9. Revise outline and aids

10. Present

11. Seek feedback on performance

Did you manage to complete the presentation within the time limit? If not, why not?

Did you hold the audience's interest? If not, why not?

Was the audience able to follow the presentation? If not, why not?

Was the audience able to note down your main points? If not, why not?

Did you answer the audience's questions effectively? If not, how could you do so next time?

How could you improve the presentation next time?

12. Review learning

Did you succeed in improving the aspect of presentation singled out at Step 2?

What aspect of presentation will you concentrate on improving next time?

What have you learned from performing this task?

REVIEWING DISCUSSION: CHECKLIST 3

PART 1 THE INDIVIDUAL

1. Was the discussion satisfactory? If not, why not? YES / NO
2. Did you *think, plan and rehearse*[1] in preparation
   for the discussion? YES / NO
3. Did you ask for clarification when you did not
   follow a point? YES / NO
4. Did you manage to make the points you noted
   down beforehand? If not, why not? YES / NO
5. Did the other group members understand the
   points you made? YES / NO
6. Did you correct any misunderstanding of your points? YES / NO
7. Did the discussion deal with the points you
   made? If not, why not? YES / NO
8. Is there something you wish you had said?
   Why did you not say it at the time? YES / NO
9. Did you gain anything from the discussion?
   (For example, has it clarified or extended your
   thinking on the topic?) YES / NO
10. What could you do next time to make
    for a better discussion? ....

    ....

    ....

    ....

    ....

PART 2 THE GROUP

11. Did the group manage the discussion effectively? YES / NO
12. Did all group members feel they had the
    opportunity to contribute? YES / NO
13. Did the discussion develop a shape or sense
    of direction? If not, why not? YES / NO
14. What could the group do next time to make
    for a better discussion? ....

    ....

    ....

    ....

    ....

[1] See pages ix and x in Introduction

OBSERVATION SHEET 1

INSTRUCTIONS FOR THE OBSERVER

Before the discussion: Write the name of one member of your group in each corner of the box below to represent the group's seating arrangements. Do not write your own name in the box.

During the discussion: Each time that someone speaks, draw one or more arrows to show the addresser (i.e. the person who spoke) and the addressee(s) (i.e. the person(s) to whom the addresser spoke).

OBSERVATION SHEET 2

INSTRUCTIONS FOR THE OBSERVER

Before the discussion: Write the names of the members of your group (excluding yourself) in the first column of the table below, one in each box, in the order in which they are sitting.

During the discussion: Each time that one of them speaks, put a mark (/) in the appropriate box, according to whether he/she asked a question or made a statement.

NAME	ASKS A QUESTION	TOTAL	MAKES A STATEMENT	TOTAL

After the discussion: Add up the total number of questions and statements for each person, and write the numbers in the appropriate boxes. Prepare to report to each member of your group how many questions he/she asked and how many statements he/she made. In addition, ask each group member the following questions:
1) In the discussion, did you make the points that you noted down beforehand?
2) If not, why not?

SEMINAR INSTRUCTION SHEET

As part of each session, one member of the class will report on his/her reading of one of the prescribed texts. Your report should last no more than 20 minutes, and should consist of:

1) **Brief summary** of the main points of the article. (All other members of the class will also have read the article, so there is no need for a long exposition here.)

   Your aim: to help the audience recall the content of the article clearly.

2) **Critical comments on the text** in the light of your own experience and/or other reading.

   Your aim: to give a perspective on the article and the issues it raises; to get other people thinking and give them something to respond to.

3) Identification of one or two **key questions for discussion** by the class in groups.

   Your aim: to provide a stimulating focus for group discussion.

GIVING FEEDBACK EFFECTIVELY

Give feedback that is:

- **Specific:** refer to specific aspects of the speaker's performance.
- **Constructive:** focus on what the speaker is able to improve, not on things he/she can't change.
- **Encouraging:** comment on strengths as well as weaknesses. (Some people like to start and end their feedback by commenting on a strength; others prefer to comment first on two or three strengths and then on two or three points to improve.)
- **Limited:** don't overload the speaker with more feedback than he/she can use.
- **Selective:** don't just mention everything you noticed; don't mention something simply because it is an easy teaching point; select the point(s) that affect(s) the quality of the speaker's performance most significantly.
- **Practical:** suggest what action the speaker could take in order to make the desired improvement.

REFERENCE SECTION 4

LANGUAGE HELP

INTRODUCTION TO LANGUAGE HELP SECTION

The Language Help Section is designed to help you utilise and systematically expand your spoken language resources for academic study in English. It lists useful expressions in fourteen of the key functional areas that learners have most frequently asked about, or had problems with, during the trialling of this course.

The expressions given will help you to carry out tasks on this course. However, they are not intended to be exhaustive. We strongly advise you to get into the habit of looking and listening out for other useful expressions in these functional areas. Use the space provided on each page to record them. If necessary, ask your teacher for some guidance as to how you can extend the Language Help Section.

LIST OF ABBREVIATIONS

The following abbreviations are used in the Language Help Section:

ADJ	adjective	N	noun
ADV	adverb	NP	noun phrase
cf	compare with	VB	verb
i.e.	that is, in other words	VBing	the –ing form of the verb
INF	the infinitive form of the verb		

AGREEING AND DISAGREEING

Agreeing

- *Yes, that's right.*
- *That's a good point.*
- *That's what I feel, too.*
- *I think so, too.*
- *Exactly.*
- *I (fully) agree with you.*
- *X put it very well (when he said …).*
- *X raised some important points.*
- *I agree entirely.*

Disagreeing

- *Well, you have a point there, but …*
- *Perhaps, but don't you think that …?*
- *I see what you mean, but …*
- *Certainly it's true that …, but on the other hand …*
- *I don't agree.*
- *I don't think so.*
- *That's not the point/question/problem.*
- *But what evidence do you base that on?*
- *That's no proof.*
- *But surely …?*

ASKING FOR CLARIFICATION

- *I'm afraid I didn't follow your point about ... Could you go over that again?*
- *Could you go over what you said about ...?*
- *Could you explain what you meant when you said that ...?*
- *Could you give an example of (what you meant by) ...?*
- *Could you expand a little on what you said about ...?*
- *Could you be more specific about ...?*

ASKING QUESTIONS AFTER A PRESENTATION

1. Making your question clear.

One way of making sure that a post-presentation question is clear is to indicate the subject area at the beginning of the question. To do this, start with a phrase such as the following:

- *I would like to ask something about x. ...?*
- *I have a question about x. ...?*
- *You mentioned x. ...?*
- *You referred to x. ...?*

Examples

I would like to ask something about traditional food in the UK. Is it true that not all puddings are sweet?

I have a question about the UK constitution. Does the monarch have any real power?

You mentioned some political differences between England and Scotland. Do people in Scotland want to separate themselves from England?

2. Pursuing a question

If you are not satisfied with the answer you receive to your question first time round, you may want to persist by using one of the following:

- *Sorry, I'm still not quite clear about ...*
- *That's not really what I was asking. My question was about ...*
- *Perhaps my question wasn't clear. What I'd like to know is ...*
- *I see what you mean, but don't you think that ...?*
- *I see your point, but ...*

CAUSE AND EFFECT
(past time reference)

X *was the result of* Y.
X *was caused by* Y.
The cause of X *was* Y.
One of the main causes of X *was* Y.

Y *produced* X.
Y *resulted in* X.
Y *led to* X (suggests a relatively indirect relationship).
Y *contributed to* X (indicates that Y was one of several causes of X).
Y *was a factor in* X (indicates that Y was one of several causes of X).

Note: In all the constructions listed above, Y represents the cause and X represents the effect.

Exercise
It is sometimes necessary to show that you are not absolutely certain about the cause/effect relationship.
1. In this context, what is the difference in meaning between *may, may well, may possibly* and *may conceivably*?
2. Practise adding *probably* or *may* to each of the expressions listed above.

COMPARISON AND CONTRAST

Similarities

Broadly speaking, X *and* Y *are very similar. In both cases, ...*
There are many similarities between X *and* Y*. (I suppose) the most noticeable of these is ...*
One similarity between X *and* Y *is that they both ...*
Neither X *nor* Y *...*
Both X *and* Y *...*
The incidence of N *is similar in* X *and* Y*.*

Differences

In some respects, X *and* Y *are similar: ... However, there are also a number of important differences*
between them: ...
X *differs from* Y *in several respects: firstly, ...*
In contrast to X*,* Y *...*
... (in X*), whereas ... (in* Y*).*
Unlike X*,* Y *...*
X *is (rather) more (ADJ) than* Y*.*
    (much) less
    (far)
N *is more common in* X *than* Y*.*
       widespread
The incidence of N *is greater in* X *than in* Y*.*

Note

1. The word *counterpart* is often used in comparisons:
   A recent survey revealed that British teenagers watch far more television than their Chinese
   counterparts (<u>or</u> than their counterparts in China).
2. In the above examples, the letters X and Y represent the two entities being
   compared. Thus in Unit 4, for instance, their place would be taken by the
   names of the two countries under comparison, or by phrases such as
   British families ..., whereas those in China ...

Exercise

Which of the two sentences below is correct?
   Traffic in England tends to be very heavy whereas Ireland is relatively light.
   Traffic in England tends to be very heavy whereas in Ireland it's relatively light.

DEDUCTION

1. *This* *can't be*   *the first*   *one.*
          could be   *next*
          might be   *last*
          may be
          must be
          is probably

Note

I think this could be ...	(correct)
I think this must be ...	(correct)
*I think this can't be ...	(incorrect)

You have to transfer the *not* to the first verb, thus *I don't think this can be ...*
That can't be the first one, because ...
I don't think that can be the first one, because ...

2. The word *necessarily* is also useful in the context of deduction:
   That isn't necessarily the first one. It could (equally) be the last one.

DESCRIBING AN OBJECT

Describing

- *It's called a/an …*
- *It's a tool/machine/device/thing for VBing … (with).*
- *It's (used) for VBing… (with).*
- *It's used to VB with.*
- *It's made of …*
- *It consists of two/three/four parts: …*

Example

As I haven't got the actual object with me here, I have had to bring in a photograph of it to show you. It's called a briki, and it's used for making coffee in the traditional way. As you can see, it's made of metal, and it consists of two parts: a small, conical pot with a long thin handle. The use of the briki dates back at least 600 years and its basic design has altered very little over that period. The particular briki in this photograph is something of an heirloom as it used to belong to my mother, who then passed it on to me when I got a flat of my own …

Exercise

Among the aspects of an object that you may want to refer to when describing it are its shape, the material(s) it is made of, and its constituent parts. In the above description of the briki there is at least one word describing each of these aspects: identify the words, write them in the appropriate space below and then try to add at least five other words to each category.

Shape:

Materials:

Constituent parts:

Defining

The usual construction for a short, formal definition is as follows:

Word to be defined	Verb(Be)	a/an	General class word	Defining characteristic(s)
A square	is	a	figure	which has four equal sides and four right angles.
Socialism	is	a	political system	which aims at public ownership of the means of production.

DESCRIBING TRENDS

1. Notice the two alternative constructions:

   There has been a slight rise in X in recent years.   (= *There* BE *a/an* ADJ N *in* X)
   X *has risen slightly in recent years.*   (= X VB ADV)

verbs:	*fall, decline, drop, decrease, go down/rise, grow, expand, increase, go up*
nouns:	*fall, decline, drop, decrease, downturn/rise, growth, expansion, increase, upturn*
adjectives:	*slight, gradual, steady, sharp, steep, marked, dramatic*
adverbs:	*slightly, gradually, steadily, sharply, steeply, markedly, dramatically*

2. There is a difference of emphasis between *slight* and *steady* or *gradual*. All three refer to a comparatively small change. However, *steady* and *gradual* emphasise the fact that this change continued at about the same rate for an extended period.

3. The words *peak* or *high point*, and *trough* or *low point* (all of which are nouns, *peak* also being used as a verb) are also very common in describing trends:

   There were two troughs in twentieth-century immigration to the USA; they occurred in the early twenties and the late forties.

   The population of London increased dramatically in the nineteenth century, peaked at about 8.5 million in the early 1950s, and has since fallen away to about 7 million.

4. Notice the two possible constructions after the word *trend*:

In recent years the trend has been	*for management and unions to co-operate more.* (= *for* NP *to* INF)
	towards more co-operation between management and unions. (= *towards* NP)

Exercise

Graph 1

1. There was a ------------- ------------ in production between 1950 and 1960.

2. Production ------------- ------------ between 1950 and 1960.

Graph 2

3. Consumption ------------ ----------- between 1960 and 1980.

4. There was a --------------- --------------- in consumption between 1960 and 1980.

Graph 3

5. Inflation ---------- ----------- after 1960, --------------- at --------------- in 1970.

   It ---------- ----------- ----------- since then.

Graph 4

6. ---

GRAPH 1: TIMBER PRODUCTION

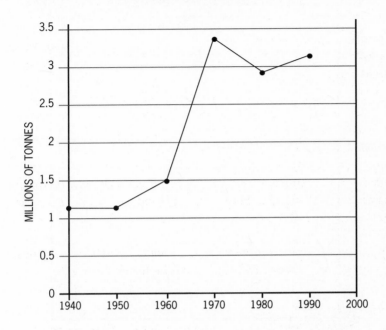

GRAPH 2: CONSUMPTION OF BOTTLED WATER

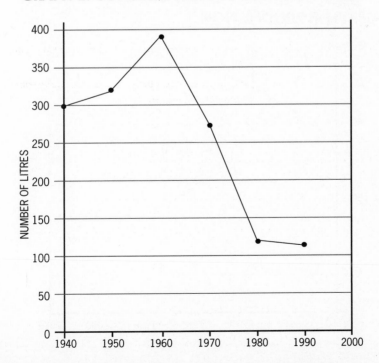

GRAPH 3: INFLATION

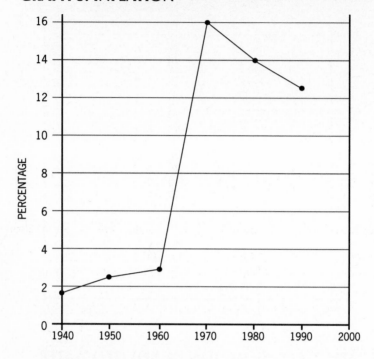

GRAPH 4: PRODUCTION

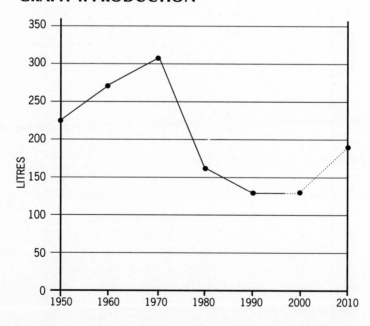

EXPRESSING OPINION

It is, of course, very common for someone to express an opinion simply by stating it, i.e. **without** using an introductory phrase such as *In my opinion*. However, these phrases are naturally used when the speaker wants to emphasise that he is not claiming the status of fact for the view he expresses:

- *My (own), (personal) view (on this matter) is that ...*
- *Personally, I think that ...*
- *It's my belief that ...*
- *The way I look at it is this: ...*
- *As far as I can see, ...*

Another way of introducing one's own opinion is to state a contrasting opinion first:

- *It is sometimes said that ..., but my own view is that ...*
- *It is widely believed that ... However, personally, I think that ...*

Other expressions give more information about the speaker's attitude to the view expressed:

- *There is some evidence that ...*
- *I understand both | sides of the argument, | but on balance I think that ...*
  | points of view, |
- *I don't think there can be much doubt that ...*
- *There is no doubt that ...*

EXPRESSING PROPORTION

1. The following pattern is common when summarising findings or describing a pie chart or bar chart.

PROPORTION	WHOLE	ATTRIBUTE
None of	the students in this class	smoke(s) more than 10 cigarettes a day.
Only about 5% of	the women in this age group	gave 'housewife' as their occupation.
A small proportion of	the British population	favour(s) withdrawal from the European Union.
1 in 3 of★	those in full-time education	
More than half (of)	the people we spoke to	
Three quarters of	the cases we examined	
The great majority of	the insects of this kind	
Almost all (of)	the people below the age of 60	
Virtually all (of)		
All (of)		

2. For reporting survey findings:

The survey revealed that   *hardly any of the respondents …*
We found that   *only a small minority of respondents …*
     the great majority of respondents …

Most of   *the respondents …*
     those questioned …
     the sample …

The people in our sample tend¹ (not) to INF.

They were evenly divided on this question (between those who disapprove of X and those who support it).

The response to this question was unanimous.

On the question of …, 60% were in favour, 20% against and the remaining 20% were undecided.

Exercise

1. What restriction is there on the use of the expression of proportion which is marked with an asterisk★ above?
2. Match each of the expressions of proportion below with the equivalent percentage figure.

around one third   *of the students in this class*
over three quarters   *of the population of this city*
about two thirds
exactly one in ten
nearly one fifth

| 10% | 77% | 18% | 30% | 65% |

3. Make some complete, true sentences with the expressions from 2.
   For example, 'Around one fifth of the students in this class speak Arabic.'

[1]Note the constructions with *tend* (a verb) and *tendency* (a noun):
   The people in this group tend to be suspicious of alternative medicine.
   There is a tendency for the people in this group to be suspicious of alternative medicine.

REFERRING TO A TEXT

- *The text is (mainly) concerned with* NP
- *The main point made in the text is that ...* + clause
- *The text   says* | *that ...* | + clause
  explains
  claims
  implies
- *According to the text, ...*
- *The view expressed in the text is that ...* + clause
- *As far as I can tell from the text, ...*

REPAIR EXPRESSIONS

These expressions can be used to prevent communication from breaking down.

In the speaking role

1. Checking that the other person has understood you:
    - *Have you got that?*
    - *Are you with me (so far)?*
    - *Is that   all right?*
              clear enough?

In the listening role

2. Asking the other person to adjust the way he/she is speaking:
    - *Could you speak up (a little)?*
    - *Could you slow down (a little)?*

3. Asking the other person to repeat or paraphrase what he/she has just said:
    - *I didn't follow that.*
                  what you said about X.
                  the bit about X.
    - *Could you say that again?*
    - *Could you repeat that?*
    - *Could you go over that again?*

4. Asking for further information to help you understand a word or phrase:
    - *What does* X *mean?*
    - *How do you spell* X?

5. Summarising to check that you have understood what the other person said:
        So, …
        In other words, …
        So, you're saying that …
        So, what you're saying is that …
        So, if I've got this right, …
        Just to make sure I've got that, …
        If I could just   recap a moment, …
                          go back over that, …

RESPONDING TO QUESTIONS

1. When you do not want to deal with the question immediately:
    I'm coming to that in a minute.
    I'd prefer to deal with that point later.

2. You can gain some thinking time by starting your response with an expression such as:
    Yes, (I think) that's an interesting question...

3. Restating the question.
    If you think some of the audience may not have heard or understood the question (because, for instance, it was asked quietly, or was long or complicated), you may want to restate the question as clearly as possible before starting your answer, as in the following examples:

    3.1 'I'd like to ask what you think is the most effective treatment for this condition?'
    → What is the most effective treatment for this condition?

    3.2 'You referred to a fall, quite a dramatic fall I think, in the mortality rate during the nineteenth century in Britain, despite the very poor living conditions in the new industrial cities. Why did that happen?'
    → Why did the mortality rate fall in nineteenth-century Britain?

    3.3 'You referred at the beginning to several different varieties of this fruit that grow in Africa and South America. But then, when you talked about the food production process, you only mentioned one variety. Was that just an example? What about the other, smaller varieties – can they be processed as well, in the same way?'
    → Can the smaller varieties of this fruit be processed in the same way?

    3.4 'You said that Western governments have been very slow to put 'green' environmental policies into action. You said, for example, that they have been irresponsible in doing so little to reduce global warming over the last fifteen years. But surely the fact is that there is still a lot of disagreement amongst scientists about whether global warming is actually taking place. There isn't enough evidence for us to be sure that the phenomenon really exists, is there?'
    → What evidence is there that global warming is taking place?
    OR → Is there enough evidence for us to be sure that global warming is taking place?

SIGNPOST EXPRESSIONS

1. **Introducing the topic**
   The subject of this talk/presentation is …
   I'm going to talk about …
   My topic today is …

2. **Preliminaries**
   I'll be happy to answer any questions afterwards.
   If you have any questions, I'll do my best to answer them at the end.
   Perhaps I should clear up one point before I start: …

3. **Outlining the structure of the presentation in advance** (= giving an overview)
   I'm going to deal with three aspects of this subject: first I'll talk about …
   I'm going to divide my talk into three sections.

4. **Indicating the start of a new section**
   The next aspect I'd like to consider is …
   Moving on now to …
   Turning next to …
   I'd now like to turn to …
   That brings me to my next point: …
   The second question I'd like to discuss is …

5. **Referring to visual aids**
   As you can see in this chart, …
   This diagram shows that …
   If you look at this map, you'll see that …
   In this diagram, X represents …
   You can see from this chart that …
   It is clear from this graph that …

6. **Concluding**
   So, to sum up, …
   In conclusion, I'd like to reiterate/emphasise that …
   So, to remind you of what I've covered in this talk, I started by VBing …
   So, we've looked at …, and we've seen that …
   Unfortunately, I seem to have run out of time. I shall therefore conclude very briefly by saying that …